I0109966

The Design Comedy

—

The Descent Through Inferno

By Otto von Busch
Foreword by Nicola Masciandaro
Commentary by Aaron Sechler

The Soul I Took from You Was Not Even Missed[1]

Nicola Masciandaro

Driven out of society by technological and media existence, and then out of the University itself . . . culture is cast into a clandestine underground.

— Michel Henry,
Barbarism

Design [*Di-segn-o*] . . . is the true sign [*segno*] of God [*Dio*] in us.

— Federico Zuccari,
Idea of the Painters, Sculptors, and Architects

There is an intimate relationship between modernity and hell. Where medieval culture perfected the theory of hell, the modern world has excelled in its practice—no less externally in the serial production of expanding hellscapes than internally in unsurpassed levels of mental suffering. Two sentences by E. M. Cioran express both sides of the situation. "Even when they desert hell, men do so only to reconstruct it elsewhere."[2] "It is our modern specialty to have localized hell in ourselves."[3] The historical translation of hell from being "the second death" (*Inferno* 1.117) of an immortal individual, someone's terminal deprivation of the presence of eternal or superessential Life, to being the state of living in humanity's self-made world is legible as the inheritance consequent upon

---

1 Black Sabbath, "Lord of This World," *Master of Reality* (Vertigo, 1971). Other verses from the song cry out in italics below.
2 E. M. Cioran, *The Trouble with Being Born*, trans. Richard Howard (Seaver, 1976), 82.
3 E. M. Cioran, *A Short History of Decay*, trans. Richard Howard (Arcade, 2012), 135.

the murder of God.[4] For this inheritance, following the same unitarian logic of justice seen in the Dantean *contrapasso*, is nothing but the self-murder of the human, the negation of one's divinity or native infinity that sentences people to their separative, temporary selves.[5] As Michel Henry states: "Hence the murder . . . is accomplished, which gives the murderers the possession of the world. And in the accomplishment of that murder, humanism is born in which humans make themselves their own possession, manipulating everything, including themselves, according to multiple possibilities offered to them in the world and within themselves."[6] *Lord of this world / Evil possessor / Lord of this world / He's your confessor now!* The desertion and uprooting of hell—with the whole immanent-transcendent Tree of Life that grows with it—leaves the human in the desert of its own world, abandoned to a truly insane belief in individual anthropocentric identity that makes the experience of finite egos the only possible experience.

The intersection of being modern and being in hell is thus most easily defined as the condition or disease of living shut up within oneself, trapped in the illusion whereby, precisely due to desperate total identification with ephemeral existence, the amazing fact of life itself becomes unrecognizable. As Henry clarifies, "The illusion which makes the ego its own foundation . . . completely subverts the place where we are given to ourselves in absolute Life, namely our 'heart'. If we conceal this internal relationship to the

---

4 "God is dead! God remains dead! And we have killed him! How can we console ourselves, the murderers of all murderers?" (Friedrich Nietzsche, *The Gay Science*, trans. Josefine Nauckhoff [Cambridge University Press, 2001], 120). Cf. "This is the heir; come, let us kill him and have his inheritance" (Matthew 21:38).

5 The term 'native infinity' is intended to remind you of the so-beautiful ending of Lovecraft's *Ex Oblivione*, a paradigmatic modern vision of afterlife if there ever was one: "I knew that all sights and glories were at an end; for in that new realm was neither land nor sea, but only the white void of unpeopled and illimitable space. So, happier than I had ever dared hoped to be, I dissolved again into that native infinity of crystal oblivion from which the daemon Life had called me for one brief and desolate hour" (https://www.hplovecraft.com/writings/texts/fiction/eo.aspx).

6 Michel Henry, *Words of Christ*, trans. Christina M. Gschwandtner (Erdmans, 2002), 61, commenting on the parable of the bad tenants (Matthew 21:33–46).

divine Life in which the heart is engendered and in which it remains as long as it lives, then it becomes blind in regard to itself."[7] Confirming this, Curtius put his finger on the passage between hell and modernity in a comment on the slime-submerged souls of *Inferno* 7, the sullen who "were gloomy in the sweet air [*aere dolce*] that the sun makes glad" (7.121–2): "Today these people would be treated in hospitals. But Dante considered them sinners. If I were to sum up in two words what I believe is the essential message of medieval thought, I would say: It is the spirit in which it restated tradition; and this spirit is Faith and Joy."[8] The redeemable agent is now a curable patient. *You think you know but you are never quite sure / Your soul is ill but you will not find a cure.* What was grasped as a spiritual responsibility or active-contemplative labor of the individual (the conversion of suffering into joy) is now conceived as a technical problem to be fixed by others.[9]

The shift is symptomatic of the scientific basis of modern culture, its being founded in the radical belief that mathematical knowledge of material nature is the only possible knowledge, "that there is nothing other than external being and that the truth is this exteriority as such."[10] Modernity thus develops as "a form of life that is turned against life . . . A life that denies itself," one that by definition "discredits traditional forms that developed the absolute life."[11] Inversely, Dante's "sacred poem, to which both Heaven and earth have set their hand" (*Paradiso* 25.1–2),

7 Henry, *Words of Christ*, 97.

8 Ernst Robert Curtius, *European Literature and the Latin Middle Ages*, trans. Willard R. Trask (Princeton University Press, 1953), 598.

9 On the spiritual necessity of essential sorrow (i.e. sorrow that one is, over the fact one's being), it is written: "This sorow, when it is had, clensith the soule . . . And therto it makith a soule abil to resseive that joye, the whiche revith fro a man alle wetyng and felyng of his being" (*The Cloud of Unknowing* [Medieval Institute, 1997], 71). Cf. "Suffering and Joy are never separated, the one is the condition of the other. The suffering of oneself provides the phenomenological matter for the enjoyment of oneself. It produces the flesh out of which Joy is made . . . Each one passes into the other and inverts to it, Suffering into Joy and Despair into Beatitude. This play of the Absolute with itself is the real and veritable being of each one of us" (Henry, *Barbarism*, 37).

10 Henry, *Barbarism*, 63.

11 Henry, *Barbarism*, 63.

fashions a perfect eternal home for such heresy, like that of "Epicurus and his followers . . . who make the soul die with the body" (*Inferno* 10.13–4): a cemetery of tombs into which each will be enclosed with their bodies at the end of time, forever enjoying the paradox of their own immortality in the form in which they affirmed it: DEATH.[12] Meanwhile they live as all other souls in hell in a present-less temporality much like the screen-mediated lifeworlds of today. As Farinata clarifies, "'We see, as does one in bad light, the things . . . that are distant from us: so much the highest Leader still shines for us. When they approach or are present, our intellect is utterly empty; and if another does not bring news, we know nothing of your human state. Thus you can comprehend that our knowledge will be entirely dead from that point when the door of the future will be closed'" (*Inferno* 10.100–8). Like hell, modern culture is more or less history without life. *You think you're innocent, you've nothing to fear / You don't know me, you say, but isn't it clear?* In his descent to Paradise, Dante previews not only the afterlife, but the psychic structures of our present age.

The problem uncovered in this comparison is not one of religious vs. secular views of reality but the infinitely more essential matter of life's faith, hope, and love in life, as grounded in one's (mis)recognition of the invisibility or darkness of oneself: whom am I?—the originary question wherein everyone touches (and fails to by answering it) the truth and reality of life itself.[13] So the first group of souls we see after

---

12 Cf. Father Dyer's confession in *Exorcist III* (dir. Blatty, 1990) as articulation of modernity's faith (in hell/itself): "This I believe in . . . I believe in death. I believe in disease. I believe in injustice and inhumanity, torture and anger and hate . . . I believe in murder. I believe in pain. I believe in cruelty and infidelity. I believe in slime and stink and every crawling, putrid thing . . . every possible ugliness and corruption, you son of a bitch. I believe . . . in you."

13 Cf. "The Divine likeness in the human mind is most clearly discerned when it is only known that it is, and not known what it is […] what it is is denied in it, and only *that* it is is affirmed" (John Scotus Eriugena, *Periphyseon (De Divisione Naturae)*, ed. I. P. Sheldon-Williams and Édouard A. Jeauneau, trans. John. J. O'Meara, 4 vols. [Dublin Institute for Advanced Studies, 1999–2009], IV, 73). "You cannot believe in God until you believe in yourself" (Swami Vivekananda, *Complete Works*, 9 vols [Advaita Ashrama, 1991], 5.409).

passing through *Inferno*'s gate are those "whose blind life [*cieca vita*] is so base that they are envious of every other fate . . . wretches, who never were alive" (3.46–64). To look into this mirror is to see a true horror, namely, that one's own blindness *is* the face the evil, "the violence of the deliberate refusal of life to be itself."[14] But what relief to find that this blindness is willful! Among all the deep truths of Dante's hell, the legions of dark illuminations that make it for modern readers the most fascinating (i.e. self-reflective) part of the *Comedy*, this is among the deepest, the darkest, and the one that post-medieval people in their strange despairing belief in hell are most looking for: that I am, that you cannot not be, that no one's existence is accidental or superficial, only a mysteriously total and impossibly perfect manifestation of the infinite Reality that may weirdly seem to have 'created' it.[15] Medieval Christians believed *in Deum Patrem omnipotentem, Creatorem caeli et terrae* who *venturus est iudicare vivos et mortuos* and a lot of other weird things, but they also believed in themselves, in the eternal truth of their own life or soul, far more than modern people, the ones who putatively believe only in 'the world'—something whose inexistence per se is proven by the actual existence of everything else.[16] Correlatively, the medieval belief in hell was not a belief in evil, because evil, as the 'privation of the good' (*privatio boni*), has no inherent essence or being. *Your world was made for you by someone above / But you chose evil ways instead of love.* Rather, to believe

---

14 Henry, *Barbarism*, 139.

15 *Weirdly* because "A body came into the world, but it wasn't you" (Howard, *Your Power of Natural Knowing* [New Life Foundation, 1995], 164), or as Henry says, "Creation is always an extrinsic creation, placing what it creates outside of itself . . . That life is foreign to this and to any possible exteriority, that nothing separates it from itself, that it would never be outside of itself because when, ceasing to experience itself by itself, it would cease to be life: that is what removes it from the principle of any possible creation. *Life is uncreated*" (*Words of Christ*, 84).

16 "There are planets, my dreams, evolution, the toilet flush, hair loss, hopes, elementary particles, and even unicorns on the far side of the moon, to mention only a few examples. The principle that the world does not exist entails that everything else exists . . . everything exists except one thing: the world" (Markus Gabriel, *Why the World Does Not Exist*, trans. Gregory S. Moss [Polity, 2015], 1).

in hell is to know the dimension of tragedy, and thus no less to affirm the sweet experiential truth of "every true tragedy: the solace that in the ground [and underground] of things, and despite all changing appearances, life is indestructibly mighty and pleasurable."[17]

But you have picked up *The Design Comedy*, not Dante's poem. What did your spirit, wayfaring in the dark wood of this world, spontaneously reach for when opening this book? What shipwreck brought you to this shore? *You're searching for your mind don't know where to start / Can't find the key to fit the lock on your heart.* Think about it and let me slow down just a little those rising stars to consider one perspective from which the mirror between hell and modernity sheds light on Otto's infernal quest for the divine spark of design, the "labor of soul, the shaping of life."[18]

The modernity of design, its complicity with the scientistic denial of life and exaltation of spatio-temporal exteriority, has historical roots in Dante's *Inferno*. In the same year (1588) that Federico Zuccari was completing his most beautiful illustrations of *The Divine Comedy*, Galileo Galilei, the inaugurator of the "inconceivable divergence between knowledge and culture"[19] in the modern world, was presenting two lectures to the Florentine Academy entitled *On the Shape, Location, and Size of Dante's Inferno* which secured him a professorship in mathematics at the University of Pisa.[20] The conjunction is telling.

---

17 Friedrich Nietzsche, *Birth of Tragedy*, trans. Roland Speirs (Cambridge University Press, 1999), 39, punctuation modified.

18 It is proper to speak of the poet, like Dante, on a first name basis.

19 Henry, *Barbarism*, xiv.

20 See Galileo Galilei, *Due lezioni all'Accademia fiorentina circa la figura, sito e grandezza dell'inferno di Dante*, https://it.wikisource.org/wiki/Autore:Galileo_Galilei. Zuccari's illustrations are available here: https://www.uffizi.it/en/online-exhibitions/dante-istoriato-hell.

Zuccari designs, which he kept with him through-out his life, manifest a deep sympathy with Dante's visionary text—"both were obsessed with the idea of design as communicating the divine to the human, and vice-versa"[21]—and the experience of translating his imagination of the poem into drawings must have permeated his subsequent radical theorization (as president of the Academia del Disegno in Rome) of *disegno* as the integral creative process of a "spark of divinity" [*scintilla della divinità*] as it passes in "un-interrupted continuity" from "an image in the mind" to "the material pencil in his hand" to "a drawing on paper."[22] Galileo's interest in the *Inferno*, on the other hand, was geometric and architectural, concerned with calculating quantitatively the spatial dimensions and structure of Dante's "infernal theatre" without regard for the souls who fill it.[23] *You turn to me in all your worldly greed and pride / But will you turn to me when it's your turn to die?* Here "Dante commentary and mathematical physics . . . become, for a moment at least, the same thing."[24] This is a strange place to be in, neither the ethical and intellectual sphere of interpretive exegesis nor the observational and epistemological landscape of natural philosophy—and both at once in a dark creative matrix that did give birth to "something unexpectedly deep," namely, the laws of scaling.[25] The strangeness becomes more haunting when we consider how the lectures' open-ing reads like an allegory of the new world of science, the soulless architectural underworld of the "Galilean

21 Tim Smith-Laing, "Dante has stumped many an artist—but these delicate drawings are truly divine," *Apollo: The International Art Magazine*, 1 February 2021, https://www.apollo-magazine.com/dante-divine-comedy-illustrations-federico-zuccari-uffizi-florence/.

22 Moshe Barasch, *Theories of Art, 1: From Plato to Winckelmann* (Routledge, 1985), 299, 302. On the historical background, see Claire Robertson, "Federico Zuccaro's Accademia del Disegno and the Carracci Accademia degli Incamminati: drawing in theory and prac-tice," in *Römisches Jahrbuch der Bibliotheca Hertziana* (Hirmer Verlag, 2012): 187–223.

23 Galileo, *Due lezioni*, Lezione I.

24 Mark A. Peterson, *Galileo's Muse: Renaissance Mathematics and the Arts* (Harvard, 2011), 236.

25 Peterson, *Galileo's Muse*, 233.

reduction" of reality to the objective measurable universe, wherein the "kiss exchanged by lovers is only a collision of microphysical particles."[26]

> If it is an amazing and wonderful thing that men have been able, by long observations, unceasing vigils, and perilous explorations, to determine the measure of the heavens, their motions fast and slow, their proportions, the sizes of the stars—not just the nearby ones but the distant ones as well—and the geography of the land and of the seas: things which, either in whole or in large part, are sensible to us; how much more marvelous must we esteem the investigation and description of the location and form of the Inferno, which, buried in the bowels of the earth, hidden from every sense, is known to no one by experience; where, although it is easy to descend there, it is nonetheless very difficult to return, as our Poet tells us so well: "Abandon every hope, you who enter."

In other words, the subterranean territory of scientistic modernity, the world as experienced by no one—"modern science has its origins in an unprecedented mistrust of experience"[27]—is hell, not as the spiritual torment of being deprived of divine presence or living without Life, but as the *space of design* from which nobody returns, knowable only in the self-ne-

---

26 Henry, *Barbarism*, xiv. Henry explains the "Galilean reduction" in relation to life's inner-outer sensibility: "To separate the reality of objects from their sensible qualities is also to eliminate our senses, all of our impressions, emotions, desires, passions, and thoughts; in short, all of our subjectivity that makes up the substance of our life. This life as it is experienced in its uncontestable phenomenality – this life that makes us living beings – thus stripped of its true reality and reduced to a mere appearance" (xiv).

27 Giorgio Agamben, *Infancy and History: On the Destruction of Experience*, trans. Liz Heron (Verso, 1993), 19.

gating mode of being a non-present or non-living observer. This is not the sensible hell which Dante's poem gives experience of, but as Galileo's terms make clear, the "site of the earth" that Dante "so exquisitely designed [*disegnò*]."[28] "As the stairs emerged, a sign loomed above, / Warning of realms void of mercy or love. / 'BELOW DESIGN MADE ITS DARKEST CENTER, / NOW SHED ALL HOPE, YOU WHO ENTER."[29]

The Design Comedy, by returning damnation to the hearts of designers, ingeniously inverts or sacredly profanes the Galilean paradigm. Mapping modern design's spiritual hell-states onto the shadow of Dante's *Inferno*, Otto's poem gives design back to "humanity, the gift divine,"[30] restoring it to the world of the living. In all the levels of sin we sink through, the circles of "design's collapse," what comes into view more than incisive observations of disciplinary critique are the anonymously intimate faces of specific flavors of human, suffering hearts sketched in the ink of the author's own sorrow. As we read while taking leave of the "peer-reviewed crypts" where "design [is] reduced to a conference of moaning," "I looked on with sorrow, my heart filled with guilt, / What had become of the hopes I had built? / How had I failed, been a part of this fall, / My grave I made myself, cursed and banal."[31] Throughout the text it is life's strange self-centered negation of itself, the violence committed in the name of knowledge or progress against culture's own

---

28 Galileo, *Due lezioni*, Lezione I. He uses the term only in relation to Dante's representation of hell, in contrast to the "the marvelous fabric of the heavens" which, as per the opening remark on astronomical observation, the poet "revealed [svelò]."

29 *The Design Comedy*, canto I. Cf. "The ordinary man never loses faith. He is as one who climbs up a mountain a certain distance and, experiencing cold and difficulty of breathing, returns to the foot of the mountain. But the scientific mind goes on up the mountain until its heart freezes and dies. But this mind is becoming so staggered by the vastness still beyond it that it will be forced to admit the hopelessness of its quest" (Meher Baba, *The Everything and the Nothing*, 89).

30 *Design Comedy*, canto V.

31 *Design Comedy*, canto VI.

vitality, that is indicated and diagnosed, all the way down to the sickest icy core of "Promethean dis-ign turned toxic in time," the one who weeping chews on the three traitors of tradition, solidarity, and hope.[32] This is not the world we want. Nor is it the one we live in. "We want selfless design *in life*."[33] Haloed in the playful exegetical glow of swerving headbanging glosses, anti-blindness sparks from the subterranean forge where the culture of life continues to labor and survive in clandestine form, *The Design Comedy* sings the design-tragedy of modernity in a spirit of faith and joy, reopening our hypocritical, all-too-human gloom to "the sweet air that the sun makes glad." Read it for life, for pleasure, "the emerald wisdom."[34]

---

32 "One mouth chews the traitor of tradition, / Scorned past lessons in reckless ambition. / Another chews through solidarity's thread, / Where bonds of the many were left for dead. / The third mouth grinds hope's betrayer to dust, / Who promised the world, but broke its trust" (*Design Comedy*, canto XIII).

33 Princess Norina Matchabelli, "Manifesto: To All Who Seek Life and Light (1936)," *Awakener Magazine* 17 (1977): 24, my italics.

34 *Design Comedy*, canto XIII. Cf. "It's all rotten. I feel it in the air and in the people frightened and starving huddled in a crowd. But I believe that in the depths of rottenness there exists—green sparkling redeeming and promised-land—in the depths of the dark rottenness there shines clear and captivating the Great Emerald. The Great Pleasure" (Clarice Lispector, *A Breath of Life*, trans. Johnny Lorenz [New Directions, 2012], 155).

CANTO
I

¹ Past midway on the journey of my days,
I lost myself within a relentless maze.
Dark corridors of design school's halls,
Where unlit offices occlude the walls.

⁵ Classroom doors locked out of sight,
My tools estranged in their depths of night.
I wandered lost, in anguish and deep despair,
No prospect but stale, institutional air.

⁹ I sought the stairs, to climb the woodshop to start,
But alas! Here appeared a leopard, fierce and smart.
Its white hide, every move held fast,
Each step I took, it blocked, until I passed.

¹³ Another stair, my hope began to swell,
But there a stygian lion stood, a beast of hell.
Its hunger endless, its eyes a fiery glare,
I fled down again, turned by its stare.

² **Maze:** See *A Maze of Death*, the 1970 Phillip K Dick novel where the crew of a doomed spaceship share a joint hallucination to allow them to painlessly await rescue while their ship hopelessly circles a dead star. The ship is called Perseus 9, which makes this the first of many classical references to follow.

³ **Dark corridors etc:** The deliberate omission of the article "a" identifies the author as a non-native speaker of english, who may be able to use his distance from this culture to see it for what it is.

⁶ **Tools estranged:** A tool becoming estranged to its user is the example Martin Heidegger uses to illustrate the process by which a craftsman becomes aware of his own being in the first division of his 1927 classic *Being and Time*. N.B. that one of the keys to understanding *Being and Time*, his lecture class of Plato's *Sophist*, given in 1925 and attended by future New School professor Hannah Arent, follows Aristotle's *Nichomicean Ethics* as treating Τέχνη (craft) as one of the five ways the soul has of accessing truth. This reference is definitely limited to these two classic texts and is unlikely to be meant to resonate with any later texts about tool being. It's also worth noting that the first two external references our author makes are to a mentally ill messianic Christian named after genitals and a Nazi.

⁹ **Woodshop:** The narrator is literally taking himself to the woodshop, a phrase often used to refer to putting farm animals out of their misery.

⁹ **Climb:** I can attest the woodshop at Parsons is upstairs, in the so-called *Making Center*.

¹¹ **White Leopard:** This is a multifaceted allusion to T.S. Elliot. The white leopard recalls both the white leopard mentioned in *Ash Wednesday*, which demands prayers for a sinner's death immediately before invoking the leopard, and Elliot's famous retort "I mean, 'Lady, three white leopard sat under a juniper tree.'" he offered when asked to explain his text to a Catholic book club. This clearly signals that what follows is likely to be opaque to the modern day equivalent of a Catholic reader and that an orthodox design academic is likely to need detailed notes to appreciate the true meaning of the text.

¹⁴ **Stygian Lion:** This is likely the stygian beast referenced in High On Fire's "Madness of an Architect" from *De Vermis Mysteris*, which opens with the line "black stygian soil conjures craft" and features cover art by legendary tattooist Tim Lehi, a modern american hero of craft who exists outside the ossified walls of the academy. The author's neighbor has two large tattoos from Lehi and the author is well aware of Lehi's supremacy in the world of tattooing, an applied craft the author is hardly ignorant of.

¹⁷ The final staircase brought no sweet reprieve,
A she-wolf barred the way, its ribs aggrieved.
So lean, so craving, full of cold disdain,
It froze my will, my heart cried with pain.

²¹ Resigned, I crumbled to the marbled floor,
No workshop keys, no pathway to restore.
The school of design, once a place of hope,
Now a tomb of a sad and powerless trope.

²⁵ But then, a shadow stirred within my view—
A spectral form, both strange and faintly true.
What stalks these corridors at night's cold hour?
A shadow, a whisper, a fleeting power?

²⁹ "Who are you, a ghost? A shade out of sight,
Or a memory lost to the depths of night?"
At first I feared, then recognition came:
The woodshop tech, Virgil, whispered my name.

---

¹⁸ **She-wolf:** The she-wolf is a clear reference to the wolf that suckled Romulus and Remus, the mythical founders of Rome. This immediately draws the reader to read the text against Virgil's *Aeneid*, a deliberate attempt to provide a politically acceptable origin story for the empire by aping literary styles that were almost eight hundred years old when the Anead was composed. This immediately opens questions into why the author would choose to use literary styles that are even further in time from him than Homer was from Virgil - does the extra hundred years distance the author needs from his source material say more about the author or the empire he is attempting to create an origin story for? Keeping the reader's nose in the classics also performs at least two more important functions. It prevents misinterpreting the character Virgil as the ghost of modern design icon Virgil Abloh. Romulus and Remus is also the ninth song on High on Fire's *De Vermis Mysteriis*, which both underscores the reference made above and shows that the text is just as interested in heavy metal as it is in its more obvious literary forbearers.

²⁹ **Shade:** The narrator is literally Calling Forth the Shade, the name of the fourth track on Necromaniac's 2025 debut *Sciomancy, Malediction & Rites Abominable* and reminding the reader of the author John Francis Shade, who composed the poem *Pale Fire* that Nabokov famously misappropriated in his novel of the same name.

³² **Virgil:** Virgil is not named until the middle of the first Canto, clearly aligning him with Aeneas, the hero of the roman poet Virgil's own epic poem. Virgil holds off identifying the hero of his epic in direct contrast to the early identification of the heroes of the Iliad and the Odyssey, and perhaps Virgil's work here will establish another Pax Romana in the craft world, where solid design rises above the intercene warfare of theory and research to create a historic period of prosperity.

³² **My name:** The narrator's unmentioned name aligns him with Dashiel Hammet's nameless Continental Op and Sergio Leone's man with no name, which puts the narrator in the same position as the detective in a classic noir piece: the extra-moral enforcer of society's norms that is only motivated by the small amount of money he earns by executing his duties. A clearer way of indicating the sense of duty that the narrator feels towards his task is unimaginable.

³² **My name:** Whether the purported author of this text, Otto von Busch, is distinguishable from the character speaking on these pages is a question well worth asking.

33 Once the jewel and the workshop's steady hand,
Now condemned by the provost's stern command.
A technician once, now cast aside,
By reorganization's ruthless tide.

37 Not a master carver, nor a seer divine,
But the working soul where all crafts align.
He spoke, "The path you seek is not so clear;
Your hands are bound by policies austere.

41 No access to the shop, for rules confound:
Your liabilities mount, no loopholes found.
Your syllabus denies such work its place,
And making yields no merit in the academic race.

45 A career in crafting things is now dead,
The Academy demands words instead."
I cried, "Without the shop, how can I strive?
What hope remains to keep the work alive?"

49 I wanted to serve, to do what was right,
But how could design stray so far from light?
I cried as my heart bore the weight of pain,
"What awaits my soul in shadow's domain?"

53 Virgil replied, "To find the workshop keys,
You must descend stairs darker than these.
Witness design's demise, all that's wrong,
The vocation's lost promise and its siren song.

---

36 **Once the jewel:** Virgil's perseverance clearly shows that you do not have to die to be a hero, a clear reference to "Hero's End," the final track in Judas Priest 1978 album *Stained Class. Stained Class* is the first Priest album to use their iconic logo and a fitting reference for the beginning of a design tract.

53 **Virgil:** Virgil is the name of the Ed Harris character in James Cameron's classic film *The Abyss,* giving our hero's companion the face of the man who had to die for Robocop to be born. Robocop is perhaps the ultimate fictional example of human/craft interface from our author's childhood, but Ed Harris didn't play the cyborg himself, and you have to wonder if the narrator is accompanied by the true face of human/craft interface.

55 **Design's demise and all that is wrong:** The initial condemnation of design comes not from the author's own mouth but from the mouth of one of his characters. See Leo Strauss's *Thoughts on Machievelli,* where he points out "Machievelli was the first to utter the evil doctrine in a book and in his own name" and spends several hundred pages painstakingly pointing out where Machievelli has spoken through Livy, Livy has spoken through his own characters, and so on. The reader must take great care to note what Otto dares to put in his own mouth and what he dares only to say through his characters. The only contemporary design theorist to speak evil in his own name is Ralf Wronsov, who will have to be reckoned with throughout the coming journey.

57 Only by the way of wisdom, this realm of pain
Can you ascend the workshop's steps again.
Through secrets of secrets, the soul's dark night,
The divine hammer's most horrid plight.

61 To infernal depths where shadows starkly press,
Dark places of wisdom, in binding powerlessness."
With trembling heart, I followed, he led,
Through hidden doors, down paths of dread.

65 "You'll find familiar sights, I know,"
Said Virgil, "you've seen places far below.
In de profundis all your failures laid bare,
Ladies of sorrow, their weights you must bear."

69 At first, I dithered, heart weighed with dread,
A heavy gloom in each thought that I fed.
I hesitated forward, still gripped by fear,
But followed Virgil down the path severe.

---

60 **Divine Hammer:** The condition of the hammer is a clear rejection of the Object Oriented Ontology proposed by Graham Harman's *Dante's Broken Hammer.*

70 **Heavy Gloom:** These two words invoke all Funereal Doom Metal, especially Bell Witch and Evoken.

⁷³ We passed crumbing corridors, rooms filled with dust,
   Where every step betrayed forgotten rust.
   Through ruined foundations, the air thick with gloom,
   The whispers faint of long-abandoned rooms.

⁷⁷ As the stairs emerged, a sign loomed above,
   Warning of realms void of mercy or love.
   "BELOW DESIGN MADE ITS DARKEST CENTER,
   NOW SHED ALL HOPE, YOU WHO ENTER."

⁸¹ In darkness surrounded, my chest choked in shade,
   We walked down, as the walls to blackness fade.
   Where light is silent, our weary feet did tread,
   An opening formed where dusk and shadow wed.

⁸⁰ **BELOW etc:** Dante and Virgil cross the threshold of Hell at the beginning of the third canto, the author here is moving much more quickly, by compressing Dante's first three cantos into one he has taken the reader straight to hell. As the aforementioned Leo Strauss was fond of pointing out, the careful reader must be aware of what is said as much as they are aware of what is not said and focus in on any alteration in source material. Cf. the second chapter of *Persecution and the Art of Writing* for a clear statement, but that principal is at work in every single thing the guy ever wrote.

⁸¹ **Darkness:** An obvious reference to the opening lines from Bathory's self-titled 1984 album; "Beyond the mountains, Where the wind cries out its pain, Deserted valleys, Where the darkness always reigned."

⁸² **Blackness fade:** An unfortunate reference to Metallica's power ballad "Fade to Black", which demonstrates the author's willingness to sacrifice metal acumen to inclusivity. The breadth of metal references in the first canto is truly breathtaking, ranging across all genres of metal and spanning the vast majority of the author's life. My neighborly relationship with the author prohibits me from speculating on what happened to set the primal scene in 1978. See Freud's *Little Hans* and some Lacan stuff I won't pretend to understand, or why not Butler and Zizek or something.

⁸⁴ **Dusk and shadow wed:** The first canto ends with a marriage, the tradition that traditionally allowed sexual intercourse in the outmoded world view that Dante's poem embodies, which puts the reader on notice that the text intends to break with the onanistic tradition of contemporary theory by actually fucking. See *The German Ideology* by Karl Marx "philosophy stands in the same relation to the study of the actual world as masturbation to sexual love." This is the first of many indirect references to Marx, a theorist far too basic for the author to make even slightly less oblique reference to.

CANTO
II

¹ We found a garden richly gathered to meet.
   Where flowers bloomed with fragrance sweet,
   The petals, so vivid, their colors deep and rare,
   Held visions of utopias, floating in the air.

⁵ We wandered the grounds, lush and bright,
   Living in imperial mode of delight.
   Fantasizers hallucinating, praising lucid schemes,
   Dazed, chattering, in spirited dreams.

⁹ I gazed in awe, lost in their blissful grace,
   Then Virgil turned, his eyes upon my face.
   From silence deep, he broke the stillness, spoke,
   His words like pale fire, through the quiet they broke.

¹³ "Look at these designers, dazed by their wine,
   Addicted to the opium of dreams divine.
   'What could be,' an anesthetic they'd say,
   A drug that pushes reality away.

¹⁷ With lotus blooms, they'd drift in thoughts and cheers,
   Chasing ghosts of once progressive years.
   They are of times when design could heal,
   When form and function made social change real.

²¹ Now, in indolence and hope's sweet embrace,
   They still see the world as a malleable place.
   With endless capacities to explore,
   Humans shape the world, forevermore.

---

¹ **Garden:** Consider Hieronymus Bosch's triptych T*he Garden of Earthly Delights*, or, more accurately, by its dutch name, *De tuin der lusten*, meaning "The garden of lusts," a Where's Waldo of surreal performativity. The sleeve of Celtic Frost's eclectic 1987 album *Into The Pandemonium* features part of the hellscape of the top right panel. This reference underscores the author's intent to not only fuck but to fuck in the actual world, the reference to the Christian idea of worldly delights is completely without irony.

⁴ **Visions of utopias:** The narrator has left this world behind, just like the narrator in "Beyond the Realms of Death," the penultimate track on Judas Priest's 1978 album *Stained Class*.

¹² **Pale Fire:** Another reference to John Francis Shade's well known poem of the same name.

¹³ **Look at these designers:** This is a version of a scene in Dante's fourth canto, so the author is still following Dante's plan, albeit at an accelerated pace. It also alerts the reader that the number of cantos has been carefully changed.

¹⁴ **Opium:** The reference to opium should be read as an allusion to Homer's *Odyssey* and not a banal mention of Marx's famous condemnation of religion. This is confirmed by the end of this canto.

25   Opium-eaters deceived by Massive Change,
   As walls crumbled with power rearranged.
   Winds of Change the anthem of the air,
   TED-talks flourished, with all hope laid bare."

29   In the haze, freedom's cry resounded,
   A realm of hopes and futures unbounded.
   "Information wants to be free!" they sing,
   Here countercultures hailed a boundless spring.

33   "In their vision, the environment is freely gifted,
   An open field where human spirits can be lifted."
   "Possibilism," Virgil said, "is where design can find,
   The world is full of change and potential, undefined."

37   The designers in the garden ate their flowers,
   Explaining theories that held no real powers.
   "Possibilism opens endless choice,
   Design thinking gives wishes a voice.

41   Speculative futures open the door,
   Where hopes reign, and facts are no more.
   Here there are no laws, no limits, no fate,
   Causality is overruled, no need to wait."

---

27 **Winds of change:** The presence of false metal in such an idyllic setting sets the stage for what follows, there could hardly be a stronger condemnation of an intellectual practice than voluntarily listening to a Scorpions ballad.

30 **Hopes and futures:** The surprisingly hopeful turn the text takes brings to mind the emergence of Polish Black Metal in the early 90's, with Behemoth playing an important role in illustrating the unseemly profits cynics can make from appropriating authentic subcultures. Evangelion's use of simplistic riffage over admittedly impressive drumming to approximate the sound of Nile's *In Their Darkened Shrines* and *Annihilation of the Wicked* shows that cynical commercial success doesn't even oblige bad actors to stay within the same genre to drive an S Class AMG. Put another way, black metal's aesthetic can allow poseurs to profit greatly of death metal passed off as black metal without bothering to sound like the Finns. One can only hope that design has its own Mgla that will emerge from the mire of crass commercialization.

32 **Counterculture:** The endless flurry of metal references shows that the author is not against drawing on counterculture as long as the counterculture is metal.

35 **Virgil:** Virgil is the name of the character Ed Harris plays in James Cameron's classic film *The Abyss*, yet Harris also plays the villain in David Cronenberg's 2005 magnum opus *A History of Violence*, where Harris serves as the face of ill gained old money that threatens the seemingly idyllic all American existence the Viggo Mortensen character is enjoying at the opening of the film, which draws the reader's attention to the obvious sinister role that capital plays in design without making outdated references to Marx.

37 **Ate their flowers:** The designers are literally Homer's lotus eaters, and shouldn't be seen as forcing their pablum on the masses. Otto is looking past his companion's name sake to go to the source material to give the reader hope that he, and by extension design, can escape the doldrums the way that Homer's hero, the man of many designs, was able to.

⁴⁵ I asked a dreamer, "What is this place?"
He answered softly, with a distant grace:
"What is, is not the truth you need to see,
For only what could be will set you free."

⁴⁹ Virgil sneered, "Here visions of change is king,
Creativity born, deemed the brightest thing.
Design, a playground where foresight can flow,
Creative daze where only preferable fates grow."

⁵³ A dreamer with eyes full of hope turned my way,
"I love your work professor, such creative play!
You look so sad—is reality unkind?
Take these flowers, and leave your woes behind!"

⁵⁷ Yes, I thought, is design not a hopeful art,
To dream of a world with a brighter start?
What flaw could there be in wishing for more,
In dreaming of better than came before?

⁶¹ I stood there frozen, unsure what to do,
Their hopeful words, so tempting, so true.
I turned to Virgil, seeking steady ground,
His gaze was firm, his wisdom still profound.

⁶⁵ "Creative clairvoyance makes fancy take flight,"
Virgil said, "They ignore reality's fight.
A worldview of plasticity, where speech acts perform,
More potential than outcomes, they seek to transform.

⁶⁹ They scorn the engineer, the builder's hand,
Here authors and dreamers gain the better stand.
For they are opium poets, not builders of things,
Their designs speak not of use, but of wings.

⁵⁵ **Is reality unkind?:** The author unintention- ally illustrates Hegel's maxim that no man can look beyond his times by making reference to the 1994 slacker film *Reality Bites*, which also illustrates that even bastions of true metal like Scandinavia are not immune to the danger American culture presents to angsty youth.

⁶⁵ **Creative clairvoyance makes fancy take flight:** A beautiful line with an obvious reference to Iron Maiden's 1988 song "The Clairvoyant" and its Delphic role in the concert documentary *Flight 666*.

⁷² **Speak of use:** Not a reference to use value.

73 Pitch Decks and markets to sell and distort,
   Where fabulation reigns, and facts fall short.
   Tangible world, concrete and pragmatic need,
   Gives way to the dreams of an endless creed."

77 Dizzied from fragrance, sweet and heady,
   We needed to clear our heads, get our minds ready.
   The flowers, like tendrils, wrapped around the mind,
   Calling our thoughts into realms undefined.

81 We left the designers there, their visions intense,
   Fantasies of unguarded futures, in unreal defense.
   They were lost in the haze, the opium they'd swallowed,
   While the present, ignored, in shadows, wallowed.

76 **Creed:** Creed may simply mean the Christian metal band Creed and not a set of beliefs, Virgil is warning Otto of the possibility of an eternity spent listening to insipid devotional hard rock, which is the kind of hell even the most steadfast atheist metalhead is obliged to fear.

81 **We left the designers there:** The author is able to leave the lotus eaters behind the way that Odysseus does in Book IX of the *Odyssey*, but the author's refusal to make direct reference to Homer should not keep the reader from recognizing the affinity the author shares with this part of academia.

CANTO
III

¹ With Virgil leading, we climbed a dark height,
Where a cliff met a storm in the fading light.
The sky was a shroud of tempest and dread,
With shadows that twisted and wind that bled.

⁵ The gale howled fierce, a deafening roar,
It battered our steps as we pressed to explore.
Between its gusts came sorrowful cries,
Lamentations and echoes that pierced the skies.

⁹ Each wail carried pain, a grief unbound,
Answers lost through the storm's surround.
I clung to the rocks, my heart gripped with fear,
For the cries seemed to whisper, "You too belong here."

¹³ At the cliff's edge, the void stretched vast and deep,
We saw glimmering souls in stormwinds sweep.
With wings outstretched, they drifted, tossed, and blown,
Doomed never to settle, their paths unknown.

¹⁷ Virgil spoke, his voice like the wind's lament,
"Behold these poor souls, here forever bent.
Unanchored in space, unmoored in time,
Their fleeting attitude is their only crime.

²¹ They chase emergence, one project ahead,
The past forgotten, the future misread.
Their tasks ephemeral, their goals unclear,
Tied to no place, to no moment near.

---

² **Cliff met a storm:** An allusion to the fatal defenestration of Metallica's Cliff Burton on a tour of Sweden in 1986 reminds the reader of the grimm fate that often befalls false metal in Scandinavia and gives the reader a brief glimmer of hope in an otherwise bleak narrative. Burton died on my 10th birthday and cleared the path for Deleuze's defenestration almost ten years later, one can only wonder what the third term in that particular thesis-antithesis-thesis will be. See Alexandre Kojeve's *Introduction to the Reading of Hegel.*

¹¹ **Fear:** I sense the author is here referring to the curious overlap between Steve Harris' composition of "Fear of the dark" and Deleuze and Guattari's discussion on The Refrain: "A child in the dark, gripped with fear, comforts himself by singing under his breath. [...] There is always sonority in Ariadne's thread."

¹⁴ **In stormwinds sweep:** The language nicely evokes the sweeping guitars on the Dissections's 1995 class *Storm of the Light's Bane.* This is the second reference to a musician who met an untimely demise in Scandanavia, although Nödtveidt's suicide shows that such deaths are not all cases of death to false metal.

²¹ **Emergence:** The term Emergence serves as a stand in for the general kind of loose talk that plagues academia. Google Ngraph places the peak of the use of the term in 2016, so a reader could be tempted to think the author has compared himself to an amoeba or slime mold around that time. But as always, the true reference is to the classics, and the author only alludes to Motorhead's "Emergency" from the 1980 album *Ace of Spades,* where Lemmy predicts how quasi-academic lingo affects mental abilities; "They must be mad, must be blind, Driving me crazy right out of my mind"

²⁵ The aristocracy of art, who travel far and wide,
Through global circuits, in culture they reside.
As artists, architects, and scholars they roam,
Their mercenary work finds no true home.

²⁹ Here, design is no longer a steady creed,
But fleeting projects, born from reckless need.
A swirl of culture, symbols intertwined,
Chaotic, individual, and blind.

³³ In continuous orbit, their work reaches far,
Keynotes and biennales are their guiding star.
Symposia and salons where egos meet,
Collecting miles for the upgrade seat."

³⁷ The wretched souls were tossed upon the gale,
I watched them drift and felt my spirit fail.
The wind tore at my skin, my tears ran free,
A flood of shame and raw agony.

⁴¹ In deepest guilt, my rootless self was bound,
While biting winds and grief closed all around.
Then Virgil spoke, his voice a steady guide,
To pierce the storm and draw me to his side.

⁴⁵ "From trends to policies, the winds decide,
Which residencies to fly through worldwide.
But never they anchor, no sustainment they build,
Merely skim the surface; their debts unfulfilled.

---

²⁸ **Finds no home:** The reader must resist the urge to read this against Heidegger's identification of man as unheimlich in his discussion of Antigone in his 1942 lecture class published as Volume 55 of his Gesaumtausgabe, where the condition depicted so negatively here is seen as an inescapable part of human nature.

²⁹ **Creed:** You would think distinguishing anything from the most insipid band in the history of the world would be a positive, but in this case you would be wrong.

³² **Chaotic, individual, and blind:** The inhabitants of this circle of hell have put traditional craft in the position of the savages mentioned in the seventh song of Judas Priest's 1978 album *Stained Class*. Positioning a reference to the seventh track after those already made to the eighth and ninth track confirm that the author is playing the album backwards for the reader, the very same act that allegedly lead to the death of two American teenagers and the resulting 1990 trial that saw Judas Priest acquitted of corrupting the youth, a charge that earlier philosophers like Socrates were unable to beat or even deny.

⁴¹ **My rootless self:** Consider whether the author aligns himself with rootless cosmopolitans.

⁴⁹ They see the world as always becoming,
A fluid system, interbeing's plumbing.
With quick fixes, they seek to hack the flow,
Interventions with no burden to show.

⁵³ Their currency is concept, claims are vague,
Situated, positioned, yet every place they plague.
Briefly they land to extract what they need,
From roots they tear, then onwards they speed.

⁵⁷ Commons, they chant, while they live for themselves,
Elites of the system, adorning its shelves.
Luxury communists, feeding from the poor,
Scorning labor as deplorable, impure.

⁶¹ Exploited themselves, yet parasites still,
They prey on the struggle that others fulfill.
Chasing oppression to build their CVs,
While crying for justice on borrowed knees.

⁶⁵ Conflict is nectar in the grant-giving race,
And community ends when funds misplace.
Peers turn to rivals, awards keep them apart,
Collaboration's a means, not of the heart."

⁶⁹ Across the storm I heard their creed,
"Awards and impact, this credit we need."
Illusions of freedom I saw them sustain,
With no bearings their struggles were vain.

---

⁵⁰ **Interbeing's plumbing:** The author cleverly juxtaposes Heraclitus' famous dictum with the image of a Deluzian pipe coursing with feces to show that when it comes to academic design you can't even step in the same pile of shit twice.

⁵⁵ **Briefly they land to extract what they need:** These theorists are in the same position as the characters in Stephen King's 1986 novella *The Langoliers,* where passengers aboard an airplane that has inadvertently flown through a time shift find that the objects in the plane no longer obey the laws of physics and are forced to land to avoid saw tooth monsters that eat lazy children. Perhaps the author dreams of a better world where lazy theorists meet a fate darker than mockery in a satirical poem?

⁵⁶ **Roots:** The allusion to the origin of Sepultura's ill fated turn to nü metal, 1996's *Roots,* can only be seen as a negative.

⁶⁹ **Creed:** The continued repeated mention of the universally despised Christian rock band drags the narrative to a new low, adding to the exigence of this canto.

⁷³ Again their cries rose through the storm's fierce roar,
"Just another application!" they implored.
The wind consumed them, tossing through the skies,
As Virgil turned with sorrow in his eyes.

⁷⁷ "Like golden locusts, their beauty deceives,
Their projects bring ruin, a harvest that grieves.
To rest would mean their fragile wings lost,
And so they drift, forever by tempest tossed."

⁸¹ Seeing their plight struck deep at my core,
A guilt in my chest I could not ignore.
Virgil's gaze met mine, stern and full of disdain,
We turned to descend, where darkness held reign.

---

⁷⁵ **The wind:** The word "wind" appears eight times in this canto, which when read against the classics, creates an unmistakable connection to Manowar's 1987 triumph "Black wind, fire and steel" where "wind" is uttered twenty three times. Taken together these can only point to Matthew 8:23, where Jesus' shows authority over nature as he calms a storm on the Sea of Galilee. It is extremely notable that the initial appearance of numerology in the text puts Otto in the same position as Jesus, the carpenter and purported son of god. These themes appear with greater clarity later in the poem.

⁷⁷ **Like golden locusts:** A reference to the 2012 compilation *Molecular Genetics from the Gold Standard Labs* by important San Diego powerviolence band The Locust, who I once saw open for Slayer. This magnanimous reference shows the author's commitment to inclusivity by referencing bands excluded from Encyclopedia Metallum. This may also refer to the book of Exodus, which is an important part of the outmoded worldview that motivates Dante.

⁸³ **Disdain:** A play on Watain, which reminds the reader of the anti authoritarian potential that black metal continues to promise, and how different the kind of acts that get to play festivals in Scandinavia can be.

CANTO
IV

¹ We walked into a valley, dim and steep,
Where cliffs loomed high, surreal, as if in sleep.
Their forms defied all reason, dark, untrue,
While shadows cast a haze that blurred our view.

⁵ Further down the pit, we reached a hill,
Where figures strained against a task of will.
They heaved up bags—notes and cash within,
Yet spilled their load, again and yet again.

⁹ Their backs were strained, their groans loud and deep,
Their faces marked by sweat they could not keep.
Here the young men bore weights on their shoulders,
Their burden heavy, straining up sacks like boulders.

¹³ Virgil observed, "With industry's retreat,
Designers sought heights in apparent defeat.
No longer tied to the factory's physical grind,
They sought the lofty realms of abstract mind.

¹⁷ Knowledge production offered higher gain,
Less toil of hand, more technologic reign.
The craft grew distant, outcomes turned obscure,
A discourse took its place, complex, impure.

⁴ **Shadows cast a haze:** The awkward use of "cast a haze" instead of fall saves the text from an unfortunate reference to the pseudo thrash band Shadows Fall and shows Otto is well aware that what you don't say is just as important as what is said. See Leo Strauss *Persecution and the Art of Writing* but not his intriguingly titled essay "On a Forgotten Kind of Writing" in *What is Political Philosophy? And Other Writings,* which failed to produce a single useful quip.

⁸ **Yet spilled their load, again and yet again:** This kind of repeated ejaculation should be read against the repeated statements about the masturbatory nature of theory and is the kind of frequent sexual activity that is prone to drawing the envy of the less fortunate.

¹⁸ **Less toil of hand etc:** Following closely on the mention of factory grind above this passage can only be read as a lament of the negative effect triggered drums have had on grindcore specifically and extreme music as a whole. The author invokes the intense discomfort a true metalhead feels when confronted with any Dimmu Borgir or Cradle of Filth recording.

²⁰ **Impure:** Otto is paraphrasing Cioran's famous dictum "True thinking resembles a demon who muddies the spring of life or a sickness which corrupts its roots," which is perplexing at first because the text appears to be criticizing design theory by calling it demonic and true, such perplexity is assuaged when the reader begins to appreciate the esoteric nature of the text.

21 Designers left solutions far behind,
    For framing issues grandly in their mind.
    Their pride grew vast, their aims stretched to extreme:
    To end all pain, reform society's theme.

25 And so, with Wicked Problems as their creed,
    They found a guise to justify their greed.
    These endless tasks, complex beyond their ken,
    Brought paid hours, requiring no action of them.

29 Problems once solved gave way to a plan supreme,
    But facing predicaments run them out of the steam.
    While problems yield to answers, fixed and clear,
    Predicaments persist, austere, severe.

33 They cannot change, but only be withstood,
    Endured in silence, as all trials should.
    Thus they play in endless, proud debates,
    Their hubris sealed their self-inflicted fates.

25 **Wicked:** A reference to the clearly stated problems in "Procreation (of the Wicked)," a song from Celtic Frost's 1984 *Morbid Tales*, calling out "Serenades of opposition, Absurdity, humans fate and hope," which forebodes the endless imitations of this album amongst generic "extreme" metal bands that use the kind of triggered drums criticized above.

25 **Creed:** One has to begin to wonder what the repeated mentions of Christian Rock are intended to do the reader, and whether this kind of repeated mockery is meant to make the true esoteric teaching of the text more difficult to reach the more of a true metalhead you are, making the text more difficult for those who are best positioned to understand it. "Those to whom such books are truly addressed are, however, neither the unphilosophic majority nor the perfect philosopher as such, but the young men who might become philosophers… Such features do not disturb the slumber of those who cannot see the woods for the trees, but act as awakening stumbling blocks for those who can." Leo Strauss *Persecution and the Art of Writing* pg. 36.

35 **Endless proud debates:** The theorists are engaging in a literal battle of the books, much like what occurs in Jonathan Swift's satirical essay of the same name. It's fitting that the first allusion Otto makes to his great forbearer Jonathan Swift is to the preface of Swift's early work A *Tale of a Tub*. Swift was involved enough in the politics of his time that it took him most of his life to create his magnum opus, the first attempt at a complete destruction of all previous thought in the English language. Otto has managed to produce a similarly ambitious text at a much younger age, possibly because unlike Swift he is not much engaged in the subject of his criticism, apart from some truly accomplished whittling. Swift was also forced to publish much of his best work pseudonymously, unlike Otto. Those who doubt the sincerity of my praise of Swift would be well served to note that none other than Leo Strauss mentions Swift in the Introduction to *Persecution and the Art of Writing*.

37 Yet the grander the issue, the sweeter the call,
    For design stands at the heart of it all.
    Wicked complexity means status and worth,
    Design at the center, remaking the earth."

41 Up the slope they push, their infinite burdens spill,
    The post-its scatter, gold rolls down the hill.
    Their task unending, their ambition vain,
    Yet full of pride to justify their strain.

45 I stood in stillness, anguish in my chest,
    Watching their struggle, no moment of rest.
    Sweat and toil marked each weary soul,
    But Virgil spoke calmly, with words of coal.

49 "In studios of thought, vision claimed the throne,
    The post-it note became the cornerstone.
    Bright scraps of paper, where desire take shape,
    Replaced the hammer, compass, and worker's tape.

53 Creativity, now sold as common gold,
    Leaving social costs in abstraction's fold.
    Solving complexity they promised to inspire,
    Yet understood little of reality's mire.

57 Ideas and brainstorm would cross any divide,
    Collective marvels where diplomacy died.
    Thus currency of thought replaced the deed,
    While Solomon's sagacity was still in need."

---

39 **Wicked complexity means status and worth:**
The author could hardly make their disdain for
Technical Death Metal and its artificial drum
sound more clear here. Leo Strauss is justly famous
for demonstrating the oblique means of expression
that authors are forced to use when persecuted,
and nothing could attest to the dire strait of academia more than an author being forced to hide a
fairly straightforward critique of modern metal in a
satirical poem that ostensibly critiques contemporary design theory. See the introduction to Strauss's
Persecution and the Art of Writing already mentioned repeatedly above and any Origin record.

40 **Earth:** Citing the seminal band Earth before
mentioning their imitators Sunn0)))) draws
attention to the latter's true status as false metal.
I have personally witnessed the author's disin-
terested response to Sunn0))))'s live show.

43 **Unending:** Much like Sunn0))))'s live show.

49 **Throne:** The image of a paper throne vulner-
able to the heat of true desire recalls the blas-
phemous title of Incantation's *Mortal Throne of
Nazarene*, underscoring the fragility of Christ in
the face of true hessians. For contrast see At The
Gates classic track "Raped by the Light of Christ"
on *With Fear I Kiss the Burning Darkness.*

61 "This is the gentry of design," Virgil said,
 "Divorced from labor, where roots have bled.
 No longer do they shape, create, or mend,
 They push ideas that never find an end."

65 A sack burst open, papers filled the air,
 Degrees and diplomas, scattered everywhere.
 Like leaves they flew across the grey hill,
 While designers toiled, their focus steady still.

69 Virgil observed, his voice both sharp and low,
 "The degrees inflate, yet onward they must go.
 For if they stop, their worthlessness is shown,
 A truth they fear but dare not to bemoan."

73 We looked on how Complexity bowed their backs,
 With sweat-soaked hands, shouldering ruptured sacks.
 Their endless toil, their groans, their sweat-streaked pain,
 Forever spent on knowledge production's vain.

77 With weary eyes, Virgil waved further down,
 Past scattered sketches, gold, and futures drawn.
 "Behold," he scoffed, "the fruits of wicked schemes,
 Design divorced from labor, lost in dreams."

81 With heavy heart, I gazed on in dismay,
 Then Virgil moved deeper, leading the way.
 Through darkness we tread, with caution profound,
 Avoiding the post-its scattered around.

---

65 **Sack burst open:** Paraphrasing sexual jokes in pseudo-victorian language is an intellectual tradition that goes at least as far back as Strauss's deservedly infamous *Socrates and Aristophanes* so I'll leave not quite well enough alone here..
68 **Focus:** Mentioning Cynic's 1993 debut *Focus* only brings the critique of later Technical Death Metal's excess into, well, focus.

76 **Sweat-soaked hands... endless toil, their groans... production:** Otto could hardly be talking about anything other than the tedious experience of listening to a modern tech-death album, even the sentence "I long for the days of Necrophagist" would be less direct.

CANTO
V

¹ Further into the depths, where shadows were vast,
We came to a forest that seemed born of the past.
Its trees were contorted, their trunks split in woe,
Writhing like claws that refused to let go.

⁵ "Beware where you tread," warned Virgil with care,
"For this is the forest where guilt taints the air.
Here dwell life's defenders, noble in name,
But their twisted ideals are the roots of shame.

⁹ Suicidal designers, to nature they swore,
Yet live off the spoils of industry's war.
They blamed extraction, but reap what it yields,
Ignoring the labor of farms and fields."

¹³ Curious, I reached for a branch near my side,
And snapped off a twig—it wailed as it cried.
A voice from the tree shouted out in despair,
"Why do you harm me? How do you dare?!

¹⁷ How typical of you, cruel wood-working fool,
To ignore my wisdom and use me as tool.
You anthropocentric despot, so mean, so blind,
All the world's suffering stems from your kind!"

---

⁵ **Virgil:** Virgil is the name of the character Ed Harris plays in James Cameron's classic film *The Abyss*, yet Harris also plays the leader of the train in Boon Joon Hoo's 2013 sci-fi neo-classic *Snowpiercer*, where the survivors of the apocalypse live on a train enabled by child labor, which is an apt if slightly obvious metaphor for the current state of fashion. The current state of fashion is the name of a set of interventions the great Ralf Wronsov staged at the Nevv School in New York City a few years ago (and the university's current logo is in turn a premonition of *The VVitch*, the 2015 folk horror film by Robert Eggers).

⁹ **Suicidal designers:** Otto once again juxtaposes design and metal. While suicidal designers are rightly critiqued here, suicidal black metalers have created an entire genre of suicidal black metal without unjustly profiting from it. See Make a Change... Kill Yourself's excellent self titled debut and the better Xasthur albums.

²⁰ **Your kind:** The author is clearly parodying Cattle Decapitation lyrics, in an attempt to both criticize metal and to subtly draw attention to their roots in the hardcore scene, a haven for pseudo-intellectual teenagers who were not culturally aware enough to listen to metal in high school.

²¹ Virgil spoke now, his tone severe,
"Come closer and see, the designers fear.
Despising their birth, their kind, their name,
Yet kept centering themselves just the same.

²⁵ They cursed society, culture, and kin,
Decrying humanity as the source of sin.
They dreamed of silence, the earth's reprieve,
Yet clung to comforts they wouldn't leave.

²⁹ Refusing their humanity, the gift divine,
For an Earth without progress they pine.
Preferring extinction to life's messy fight,
They mourned the sun but still feared the night.

³³ Reality, their vista too abundant,
Made humanity itself redundant.
Despairing of life, their hearts confined,
These were the ones who turned on mankind."

³⁷ I saw the twisted limbs of trees complain,
Their murmurs cursed in ceaseless, bitter strain.
Their pain hung heavy, haunting through the dark,
As pests and vermin gnawed their weary bark.

⁴¹ The tree writhed in pain, as pests took their feast,
Chewing on roots, from the greatest to least.
Its leaves they devoured, its bark now frail,
While toothless jaws ground, in a tortured wail.

---

²⁷ **Earth's reprieve:** The author's merciless critique of false metal continues, here focusing on the vegan straight edge scene and especially Earth Crisis, Unbroken, Cave-In et allia's sad recycling of Slayer riffs from *Show No Mercy*. See generally Hydra Head record's output that Aaron Turner doesn't play on.

³⁹ **Haunting through the dark:** It is a true testament to the oppressiveness of the current situation that the author of a tract so clearly obsessed with metal has to wait until the fifth canto to allude to H.P. Lovecraft and only makes mention of a lesser known Cthulhu mythos story *Haunter in the Dark*. For the influence of Lovecraft on heavy metal see Morbid Angel's *Abominations of Desolation, Altars of Madness,* and *Blessed are the Sick,* which serve as the obvious source of the wordless ballad on Metallica's 1984 unseemly attempt to commercialize thrash metal. Or does Otto hold off naming the true hero of the work the way Virgil withholds Aeneas' name in the early part of the *Aeneid*?

45 "Behold here," Virgil said, "the post-human brood,
    Condemning extraction, though it provides their food.
    They champion Earth while scorning the poor,
    Their words build a forest of reasons obscure.

49 They wear vegan leather, claim nature's plight,
    Ignoring the people who labor through night.
    Instead of addressing the struggles of men,
    They make up plans to 'save the planet' again.

53 To them, the biosphere's struggle is grand,
    But the plight of the people, they can't understand.
    The trees moan here, for the world they forsook,
    A new chain of being without a second look."

57 Idealizing mushrooms, spurning the people's might,
    They preach for the earth, in misguided delight.
    The agency of humans, they've cast aside,
    For post-human actants, in which they confide.

61 These designers, deluded, now rooted in pain,
    Blame the enlightenment for what they disdain.
    The more-than-human betray the same sins,
    From all-too-human delusion, it all begins."

48 **Their worlds build a forest:** This is in deliberate contrast to the world envisioned in Jack Vance's first novel *Big Planet*, where a world free of heavy metal but rich in forests leads to a focus on traditional craft. This is the same kind of rejection to the increasingly mass produced culture that motivates Phillip K. Dick, who the author alludes to above, even if an interest in a world devoid of heavy metal calls much of my reading into question.

48 **Obscure:** Few bands illustrate the crisis of contemporary technical death metal better than the bewildering mixture of genius and idiocy that most Obscura records possess. The drummer who played their show in Brooklyn a few years ago had a Lars Ulrich like inability to play the drum parts as written that was in stark contrast to the virtuosic guitar playing on display, which made it clear how so many of the people on stage had once performed for Necrophagist.

49 **Vegan leather:** Wearing vegan leather is the polar opposite of the sartorial choices Lemuel Gulliver's time among the Houyhnhnms allowed him to make, and the stark opposition between fashionable plastic and the canoe made of human flesh that Gulliver uses to rejoin humanity forces the reader to wonder whether Otto is willing to sacrifice his humanity on the altar of better formed fashion theory. See Slayer's "Altar of Sacrifice" on their genre defining 1986 opus *Reign in Blood* and Alan Bloom's "Giants and Dwarfs: An Outline of Gulliver's Travels." The latter is excerpted in the Norton Critical Edition of Swift's writing, but you can get the full version of both Bloom and Slayer with a cursory googling.

50 **They wear vegan leather, ... night·** Could there be a more direct indictment of the 90's hardcore scene in North America, where upper class white males adopted the dress of the working class without having to do anything more onerous than going to a hardcore show?

58 **Preach for the earth:** Yet another clear reference to 90's straight edge culture.

61 **Deluded:** Otto wants to say Deluzed but wisely forebears from criticizing his own masters.

64 **All-to-human:** See Nietzsche dictum; "Most people are far too much occupied with themselves to be malicious" in one of the two books called *Human, All too Human*.

⁶⁵ The trees wailed louder, their anguish profound,
Their curses like whispers that circled around.
"Not about me without me!" the branches implored,
While endlessly blaming the hands they abhorred.

⁶⁹ "Their ideas are lofty," Virgil went on,
"But their understanding of people is woefully gone.
They scorn real action, they won't organize,
Yet claim to save nature, with tears in their eyes.

⁷³ They live off industries they claim to detest,
While their projects fail and fall with the rest.
Ignoring the human, they've lost their own path,
Now they rot in this grove, consumed by their wrath."

⁷⁷ Their frozen forms, in pain they stood,
A cruel reminder of all they once could.
My heart grew heavy, my spirit weak,
For their fate seemed worse than words could speak.

⁸¹ The cries grew louder, accursing all near,
A cacophony of blame, of sorrow, of fear.
We pressed on, stepping over their weeping domain,
Leaving their twisted torment and blame.

---

⁷² **Tears in their eyes:** The author makes use
of the little known scientific fact that your tears
contain too much salt to water plants.

CANTO
VI

¹ In the darkness, we pressed on, Virgil in lead,
The air grew foul, as if death had been freed.
Smoke and ashes filled the oppressive air,
And choked my soul with raw despair.

⁵ The wind reeked with cinders blight,
Fragments of burning papers dimmed the light.
A hum of voices, in sotto voce they spoke,
Whispers of darkness, as the shadows broke.

⁹ We were upon a field of smoking graves,
Where souls were trapped in crypts of rays.
Each figure writhed within their fiery plight,
Condemned to burn, yet hidden from light.

¹³ Virgil looked down graves of eternal fire,
An academic conference—a funereal pyre.
Here burned research papers, stacked and over-wrought,
In tombs lofty claims now torched, meaning naught.

¹⁷ In mausoleums scholars gathered, ghostly in pride,
Their tongues aflame with postulations, hollow, tried.
In these burning graves, each its own little hell,
Now bodies smoldered in flames' cruel spell.

---

¹ **Virgil:** Virgil is the name of the character Ed Harris plays in James Cameron's classic film *The Abyss*, yet Harris also acts in the film version of Stephen King's 1991 mid career turd *Needful Things*, making this the first of many, many allusions to Stephen King to follow. Harris doesn't play the villain in this one, perhaps alluding to his role as the sheriff who successfully opposes a shopkeeper who embodies the menace that an overly nostalgic interest in craft can pose to small town America. It's worth noting that Harris's character is only able to temporarily defeat the devil in this case, illustrating the endless nature of the battle of the giants over being Heidegger discusses in the early part of *Being and Time*.

⁸ **Whispers of darkness:** See H.P. Lovecraft's *Whisperer in the Dark*, a part of the Cthulhu mythos narrated by a professor at the barely fictional Miskatonic University, which underlines how close current academia is to hell. This kind of guilt may be motivated by something similar to Adorno's well known statement in *Minima Moralia:* "The only responsible course is to deny oneself the ideological misuse of one's own existence, and for the rest to conduct oneself in private as modestly, unobtrusively as is required, no longer by good upbringing, but by the shame of still having air to breathe, in hell." I can attest that the air in Park Slope is just as shocking to the conscience as the air by the pool in Jameson's deservedly famous quip. See Frederic Jameson's *Late Marxism: Adorno, The Persistence of the Dialectic* or just stand behind P.S. 321 on a weekday afternoon; "The question about poetry after Auschwitz has been replaced with that of whether you could bear to read Adorno and Horkheimer next to the pool."

¹⁰ **Crypt of rays:** The souls have literally gone Into the Crypt of Rays, the first song on Celtic Frost's 1984 debut *Morbid Tales*. The reference to Gilles de Rais, Joan of Arc's body guard who turned to murdering children in black magic rituals after Joan's execution ended their first band, highlights the danger of thwarting collaborative research processes and the desperate things older musicians have to do to recapture the righteous fury of their youth. See the 90's output of Maiden and Priest, which is the aesthetic equivalent of child abuse.

²¹ Virgil spoke down to them, these Artistic Sages,
Who forged peer-reviewed crypts, ablazed cages.
He sneered, bemoaning art's loyal researchers,
Ambitious minds now hollow truth's besmirchers.

²⁵ "As factories closed, this Research arose,
On winds bearing the knowledge economy's prose.
Designers thought research could guide their way,
But in crypts of futility, vagueness turned clay.

²⁹ Art catalogs grew bloated, verbose, abstract,
As curators cloaked meaning in jargon's pact.
Design schools, not to be outdone, complied,
Dressed practice in robes of their hollow pride.

³³ Enter Academia, to save the day!
Its rules more obedient, trite, and gray.
Now the knowledge markets demand their toll—
Assimilation now chokes the experiment's soul.

³⁷ These sages claim academia's polished air,
While skillfulness squandered in despair.
Instead of forging paths both bold and new,
They keep seeking cases, well-worn and few.

⁴¹ Burning in borrowed theories, grossly stretched,
Plucked from philosophies, astray and farfetched.
French authors, and esteemed lofty names,
Now reduced to fodder in their funding games.

---

²² **Ablazed cages:** Here the author's position above the blazes inverts the Darkthrone classic *A Blaze in the Northern Sky* to show that the church of design was always already in flames by the time the author arrived.

³³ **Enter Academia:** The echoes of yet another crass attempt to cash in on thrash by Metallica are not made less damming by the commercial success of the so called Black Album and its first single "Enter Sandman." (Any other band would be forced to call a record without a title self-titled, why is the band who has pushed the commercialization of thrash to its complete and total limits exempt?)

⁴¹ **Grossly stretched:** Yet another crass sexual reference without need of explanation. See goatse if you must.

⁴² **Philosophies:** Otto refers to the profession where paychecks come from the correct contacts, discourse, and the skill of grantsmanship in virtue epistemology primed to reach conclusions deemed politically acceptable, all while garnering higher pay and more sabbatical than more deserving departments.

⁴⁵ These tombs, incestuous, their world so small,
   Glazes the stables of quantification's thrall.
   These professors earn merits only from citation,
   But practice, skills, craft? It's just passing imitation."

⁴⁹ My soul froze in anguish, leaning over a grave,
   I heard a dry murmur no fire could save.
   "Practice-led New Materialism," it cried,
   Faint words in the smoke, as the papers died.

⁵³ The smolder filled my lungs, I coughed a croak,
   Tears blurred my vision, from all the smoke.
   Seeking his guidance, searching for a peer,
   I turned to Virgil, his voice calm and clear.

⁵⁷ "Here labels reign: Object-Oriented sounds so grand,
   Practice-based still tethered the academic's hand.
   No controversies spark; all voices are tame,
   This burning field of graves, bereft of life's flame.

⁶¹ Look, no bridges between thought and hand,
   Just collapsing paper castles on shifting sand.
   Droning below, their rhetoric in smoldering fat,
   Vaults of tax-funded waste—vain, and flat.

---

⁴⁵ **Tombs:** One of the hallmarks of close reading is knowing the author's position on the subject well enough to intuit what is absent from the text as well as what is present. "Once he could hypothesize about the drift of an entire dialogue or a sufficiently complex argument, he would deduce from it the consequences that should hold in the text if the hypothesis were sound. The consequences could range from a word to an entire argument that should be present or absent from the dialogue." In this case the reader must notice the absence of the word mold in this section of the text, making it impossible for the reader to connect the dark imagery with Tomb Mold, perhaps the most effective contemporary torchbearer of 90's progressive or technical death metal active today, at least in Canada. The reader can therefore be certain of the lack of irony in this passage. The quote is from "Strauss on Plato" in Seth Benardete's *The Argument of the Action*.

⁴⁶ **Stables:** The image of shit filled stables places the author in the position Hercules was in, similarly to the way that Eva Brann of St. John's College Annapolis places Socrates in many of the translation of Plato's *Republic* where she compares the position of Socrates in the allegory of the cave to Theseus saving the founder of Athens from a chair in the underworld, which required severing his flesh and dragging him to the light.

⁵⁷ **Object-Oriented:** The reference to St. John's most famous tutor is quickly followed by one to its most famous graduate.

⁶⁰ **Bereft:** The author deliberately misspells Beherit, a subtle reminder of the way that so many black metal bands turn to dark ambient when their creative spark dies.

⁶⁵ To ideologic charades, all topics now bound
Tethered to citations, handouts, circling around.
Design, once blade sharp, now dulled by their droning,
And work reduced to a conference of moaning."

⁶⁹ I saw my own flesh burned by pages vain,
My old words like ashes, my touch in pain.
These books of effort promised guiding light,
But now smoking cinders, useless in their spite.

⁷³ No new practice born, just vanity and air,
A weightless burden, false beyond repair.
Now scorched they leave me burned and scarred,
A foolish quest, where making's use is barred.

⁷⁷ I looked on with sorrow, my heart filled with guilt,
What had become of the hopes I had built?
How had I failed, been a part of this fall,
My grave I made myself, cursed and banal.

⁸¹ We looked back at academia, crypts baked in flame,
Their tombs alight—a grim smoldered shame.
Striding away, the flames behind grew dim,
Leaving the graves of research—not empowered, but grim.

---

⁶⁷ **Dulled by droning:** The author continues to mercilessly mock the many failed attempts by SunnO)))) to give their music unearned authenticity by collaborating with second wave black metal musicians. I have personally witnessed the author bored almost to tears by their live show, which only highlighted the futility of using a later member of Mayhem to conjure the spectre of Dead and Euronymous.

⁶⁸ **Conference of moaning:** One need only turn to Marx's previously mentioned quip "Philosophy stands in the same relation to the study of the actual world as masturbation to sexual love"- to see what Otto would prescribe to remedy the onanistic academic conference.

⁸² **Shame:** The author continues to harp on missed opportunities.

CANTO
VII

¹ We reached a barren field of smoke and flame,
Where groaning souls cried out in ceaseless blame.
Each narrow pit exhaled a fiery breath,
Where souls lay buried, headlong in death.

⁵ Virgil, with sorrow, pointed to the scene:
"These are the foes of norm, of rule, of mean.
The underdog metaphysicians dwell,
Scorning all order while exhuming hell."

⁹ Blazing in misery, their feet protruded,
In endless torment, forever deluded.
"They seek the smallest victim, low, oppressed,
To frame their stance as righteous and blessed.

¹³ They rage at any structure, law, or guide,
As their own expertise slowly dried
Blame tyranny that drowns the weak in pain,
But binds the soul to 'normative' disdain.

---

³ **Narrow pit:** Making the connection between the average age of the death metal audience and the anemic size of contemporary mosh pits explicit only furthers the depth of the mockery of the contemporary death metal scene.

⁶ **These are the foes of norm, rule, and mean:** Dante's Inferno has 33 cantos, this text has 13, making this the middle canto. This then obliges the reader to notice that Dante chooses the middle chapter of his poem to reveal the beast Geryon, the winged embodiment of fraud that the narrators are forced to use to travel lower in the underworld. Otto also chose to center his text around this canto, which highlights the author's awareness of his complicity in the current state of design and clearly marks the pseudo Fouccaultian position taken by the damned in this chapter as the worst of the worst in academia. On the importance of the middle to philosophy in general and Strauss in particular see the story Seth Benardete relates about his undergraduate experience on page 412 of *The Argument of the Action*, where Benardete tells of one of his fellow students returning from one of Strauss's lectures sceptical of the importance of the middle only to have his perplexity cured by ironically turning to the middle of Montaigne's essays to find Strauss's teaching affirmed by an ancient. Only the truly elect know if that friend was Stanley Rosen, who claims to have befriended Benardete around the same time in his essay "Chicago Days," the first chapter in *Essays in Philosophy: Ancient*.

⁸ **Exhuming hell:** A clear reference to the so called Harrowing of Hell that was popular with medieval painters hoping to find immortality on 20th century album covers without realizing the metal community would be aware enough to see the expulsion of so many of the ancients from hell, the most metal of fates, as a deprivation. See Slayer's *Hell Awaits* or all of Merciful Fate.

¹² **Blessed:** Here the author invokes the ritual repetition of blessed in Mgla's "Exercises in Futility V" where tailors, woodworkers, blacksmiths, and other traditional craftsmen are ironically praised for their role in creating an "invincible stronghold adorned with death" and "calligraphed sins as are coats of arms." The latter is perhaps another reference to tattooing.

17 They fear to face their privilege or might,
   And choose the weakest to declare what's right.
   By siding with the scapegoat, they hope to escape
   The need for justice's larger, broader shape.

21 Their digging finds no peace, no pause, no rest,
   For power's shadow fills their aching chest.
   To side with underdogs is all they claim,
   Yet fear their peers might bring them shame.

25 Their focus fragments pieces into the small,
   Splinters the whole, now all parts in thrall.
   Deep below they seek the purest view,
   While alienating allies who struggle too."

29 I looked over, a voice cried from below,
   "My quest is righteous," the feet wept in woe.
   I heard the same cry from the pits all around,
   Echoing their own truth in a wailing sound.

33 Virgil turned to me, his face a mask of grief,
   "Behold their labor, endless, without relief.
   They see oppression not in powers grand,
   But in the touch of the commoner's hand."

37 A voice rose from deep within a hole:
   "Your silence is violence to my soul!"
   Virgil replied, "Quarry those depths so cruel,
   Yet your toil builds no truth, no wiser rule."

---

20 **Justice larger:** Otto would likely say that being on "the right side of history" by equating awareness with activism while participating in fantasies of social change and shaming the politically unclean is impossible especially as a well paid academic able to live in one of better neighborhoods in New York.

20 **Justice larger:** The author continues to test the patience of the elect by rubbing their face in Enter Night, Stone Brewing's ill intentioned attempt to sell lager (larger without the r) to the masses using the least authentic metal band in the history of the world.

23 **Underdog:** An important NYHC band whose members went on to close the gap between metal and hardcore during their tenure in Into Another, most notably on the song "Underlord".

33 **Mask:** See Nietzsche's myriad comments on the importance of speaking with a mask in *Thus Spoke Zarathustra*, the topic of a seminar Leo Strauss lead in 1965.

33 **Mask:** Virgil is literally wearing a "Dead Skin Mask" much the way that Ed Gein does on the fifth song on Slayer's 1990 classic *Seasons in the Abyss*.

39 **Quarry those depths:** The author is centering Mgla's fifth song on *Exercises in Futility* and its extraordinary exegesis of the corruption of crafts. There can hardly be any more redemption on this level of hell than there is joy in Park Slope.

⁴¹ He turned to me, his face etched with disdain,
"No power of people they try to sustain.
They seek atoms and actants, break all apart,
While casting blame with every bitter dart.

⁴⁵ Authority they loathe with boundless zeal,
Refusing shared rule, and still they kneel.
By undermining norms, they think they're free,
But now burn alone in powerless anarchy.

⁴⁹ They seek the weakest, smallest thing in sight,
Imagining its wings could set things right.
With Butterfly Effects rather than teams,
Civic duty fades to shallow schemes.

⁵³ Emergence is their chant, their sacred song,
And trials of classes they see as wrong.
Responsibility they cast aside,
As citizens are left to stem the tide.

⁴¹ **He:** Otto chose to name his character Virgil after the Roman poet who also serves as the companion of the second most famous Florentine writer Machievelli. Machievelli himself forcefully contrasts those who he is forced to spend his day to day life with the time he was able to spend with the ancients in the second most famous letter by a philosopher. "Thus involved with these vermin I scrape the mold off my brain and I satisfy the malignancy of this fate of mine... When evening has come, I return to my house and go into my study. At the door I take off my clothes of the day, covered with mud and mire, and I put on my regal courtly garments, and decently reclothed, I enter the ancient courts of ancient men, where, received by them lovingly, I feed on the food that alone is mine and that I was born for. There I am not ashamed to speak with them and to ask them the reason for their actions, and they in their humanity reply to me. And for the space of four hours I feel no boredom, I forget every pain, I do not fear poverty, death does not frighten me, I deliver myself entirely to them. And because Dante says that to have understood without retaining does not make knowledge, I have noted what capital I have made from their conversation and have composed a little work." Otto is still mired among the vermin in this part of his day in his poem, he has not had time to change into more noble clothes and has not yet been able to enter the ancient courts of ancient men. While this may explain why Otto was compelled to create this text it could hardly paint a darker picture of his time with the dead, while Machievelli is able to feast on his birthright the only thing that the character Otto has over his so called life is that his imagination has been able to cast his peers into hell.

⁴⁷ **Free:** Once again Otto is as careful about what he says as what he does not say, avoiding the use of the word "liberatory" despite the pall it can cast on contemporary academic discourse. As mentioned above careful reading can predict what is not in the text as well as it can predict what is the text.

⁴⁸ **Anarchy:** Invoking Megadeth's disastrous cover of "Anarchy in the U.K." on the 1988 album *So far, So good.. So what!* reminds the reader both of the danger of forced cultural references and the wisdom of the exclusionary stance Encyclopedia Metallum justifiably uses to exclude power violence because of its unacceptable reliance on the simplistic rhythms of punk rock. See Allan Bloom's clear but obvious statements about the way you can't fuck to serious Western Art Music in *The Closing of the American Mind*. Those who are sceptical about the notoriety he brought to Strauss with his infamous public statements should see the justifiably sympathetic account of Bloom's life in Saul Bellow's *Ravelstein*.

⁵¹ **Butterfly Effect:** This twofold reference to the concept from chaos theory and the insipid 2004 film of the same name shows the danger that flippant references to mass culture can pose when they stray too far from authentic metal.

57 Their world is splintered, scattered, and unbound,
No commonality, peace, or quality is found.
For in their quest to shrink the whole to parts,
They lose the greater call of civic hearts.

61 Each piece, they claim, a universe alone,
But unity's foundations they disown.
And so they drift, dismantling the whole,
Forsaking bonds that nourish a soul."

65 The cries of burning feet still filled the air,
Their agony a song of bleak despair.
I felt my heart grow heavy in my chest,
For such a sight could make a soul detest.

69 "These pits," said Virgil, "show the endless plight
Of those who hate all order, rule, and right.
With weeping legs, no truth they defend,
Soles on fire, their digging knows no end.

66 **A song of bleak despair:** Once again the author uses the rhyming couplet "air" and "despair" to bring their absence to mind, keeping the narrative grounded in Suffocation's early classics *Effigy of the Forgotten* and *Breeding the Spawn.*

73 They do it not for good alone, but for the show,
Prestige their compass, where their efforts go.
Conveniently, the underdog is their creed,
While the Topdog's handouts pay their need."

77 Their toes twitched in flames, in the scorching heat,
As they dug in the lava, no escape, no retreat.
Each in their own hole, with no hope to see,
Trapped in the fire, forever to be.

81 Behind the smoke, the burning pits still groaned,
And as we walked, their deep sorrows moaned.
I felt the ache of anguish in my chest,
For such a sight made hope itself seem less.

77 **In flames:** One need not take the mention of a band representing the Gothenburg sound as an affirmation of melodic death metal, but rather a reminder that the scene's early output, such as At The Gates' influential 1995 album *Slaughter of the Soul*, is a celebration of Bathory's enduring influence. Even crass things like In Flames admittedly enjoyable cover of "Everything Counts" on *Whoracle* can be used to indoctrinate children when their mother was raised the wrong way. Once again my personal relationship with the author prevents me from taking this too far, but suffice it to say that I am not besmirching the way this excellent man or his equally excellent spouse have raised their children.

81 **Burning pits:** Karl Sanders' explication of *Annihilation of the Wicked* acknowledges that the "The Burning Pits of the Duat" is one of the most difficult Nile songs to play: "The Burning Pits of the Duat features further collaboration with Dallas. I worked on the lyrics and Dallas set the to music. Dallas really felt that the lyrics and title unquestionably called for utter underworld sorcery - riffs so fast, chopping and iniquitous as to musically capture the sensation of being consumed in pits of fire. So Dallas went to work, and the infernal riffing he conjured was so overwhelming in its brutality and hellish in its technicality that for the rest of us to play the material correctly required weeks of intense rehearsal; not only to play the riffs clean and in time (and to legitimately nail the tricky changes), but for the drums to maintain the overwhelming 256 BPM blasting, constant quick beat changing and crazy fills." This is exactly the kind of precise reference that serves to deepen the text for the elect without hopelessly perplexing the rest of us, and as Strauss says in *Thoughts on Machievelli* "The problem inherent in the surface of things, and only the surface of things, is at the heart of things." Otto is clearly acknowledging the difficulty of accurately describing his quotidian academic life as a stroll through hell without naming names and affirming that the appearance of the word anguish two lines later is completely without the irony lesser writers would need to wield to survive.

CANTO
VIII

Canto VIII: Now that we have acknowledged that there are 13 Cantos in this poem and Otto has referenced Machievelli's *Prince* it is time to speak of the problem in the surface of things and compare the 26 chapters of the *Prince* to Otto's 13 cantos. "We may thus be induced to wonder whether the number of chapters of the *Prince* is not also meaningful. The *Prince* consists of 26 chapters. Twenty-six is the numerical value of the letter of the sacred name of God in Hebrew, of the Tetragrammaton. But did Machievelli know of this? I do not know. Twenty-six equals 2 times 13." Leo Strauss, "Niccolo Machiavelli" in *Studies in Platonic Political Philosophy*. Otto's choice of 13 cantos would then make his text unholy or the opposite of Godly, hardly a surprising statement about a poem set in hell, but it also shows how ill the fortune of anyone concerned with design is. "Thirteen is now and for quite some time has been considered an unlucky number, but in former times it was also and even primarily considered a lucky number. So "twice 13" might mean both good luck and bad luck."

Strauss, ibid. By choosing to discard twenty of Dante's cantos instead of seven Otto is denying design this kind of duality and insisting that on passing the harshest judgement possible.

What is the import of centering a design text around Machievelli, the first thinker to insist on discussing things as they are and not as they should be? Otto is not saying that design theory is in a state that resembles hell, arguing for a more realistic view of the possibilities of design, that the ideal state of design theory would be filled with references to evil music, or that design theory would be in hell in a more just world, but that design theory is *ACTUALLY IN HELL*. The text is not wishful, playful, or metaphorical, and Otto is speaking directly and quite literally despite the many layers his text presents. The problems inherent in the depth of his text are the same as the problems inherent in its surface, and he can not only demonstrate exactly why he and his fellow theorists are living in hell but provide an exact taxonomy of who is in what part of hell and precisely why.

1 We journeyed downward as the shadows spread,
   The growing darkness filled my heart with dread.
   Through murky depths, our weary steps did stray,
   Into a gorge steeped in pale decay.

5 We descended further to a dim-lit ground,
   Cloaked figures chanting, to rhythm bound.
   In gilded robes, a gleaming golden league,
   Stumbling, weeping with effort and fatigue.

9 Their voices rose in praises pure and grand,
   Hymning the virtues with every hand.
   "Be critical," their solemn songs proclaimed,
   Yet the hollow tone of their path remained.

13 "These are designers," Virgil said with disdain,
   Who design 'with' and not 'for,' to feign
   That their aim is the social, the righteous, the true,
   Yet their deeds are a farce, with motives askew.

17 They play the part of the virtuous friend,
   A helper whose wisdom will always commend.
   No longer engineers of solutions vast,
   They peddle advice with intentions masked."

---

6 **Cloaked:** A reference to the controversy surrounding the overly polished Polish metal band Batushka and the many-layered betrayal of true metal hidden under their clean production and multifaceted marketing.

12 **Hollow Tone:** The author's criticism of contemporary death metal production never abates, the unfortunately compression all too common in post Morrisound guitar tone drawing his ire in this instance.

21 He gestured toward their leaden gilded coats,
   "Behold these hypocrites," he sharply notes.
   "They march in circles on justice's quest,
   Yet serve themselves beneath their noble vest.

25 In ancient times, their ilk played the stage,
   Their poetic designs now a moral cage.
   They speculate virtues, fabulate dreams,
   But mobilize nothing; it's all just schemes."

29 I saw their sweat-drenched faces, spent and worn,
   Under leaden robes, their strength now torn.
   Their faces ached with the weight they bore,
   Tiring their critical robes ever more.

33 We gazed upon the cloaked figures in their stride,
   Slowly they shuffled, endless time to abide.
   Deep concern etched on each weary face,
   Then Virgil spoke, his voice without grace.

37 "They cloak corruption in virtuous guise,
   Yet their hollow talk is a web of lies.
   Marx's coat they wear, with prideful pretense,
   Yet serve their own interests at virtue's expense.

22 **Hypocrites:** One can hardly imagine a stronger link between the author and the ancients than his willingness to use such an archaic word in a time when it has lost all moral force. Using such antiquated vocabulary is the polar opposite of writing under persecution and shows an understandable nostalgia for a time when public discourse could still meaningfully use terms borrowed from moral philosophy.

23 **Justice:** Otto's insistence on following Machievelli by speaking of things only as they are explains his refusal to adopt ancient political theory despite the many, many classical references sprinkled throughout the text. He does not even engage in Dante's own teleological political theory, an important influence on later thinkers like Kant, Hegel, and Marx, who Otto scrupulously avoids. The only thinker in that lineage explicitly made reference to is Adorno, whose negative teleology is the darkest kind of thinking possible. Once again Otto is mired in the hell that academic design is, not wistfully treating it as it could or should be.

24 **Noble vest:** Otto's contempt for false metal pathetic battle vests of hedge fund hipsters, flashing pristine battle vests that may as well have been purchased at Hot Topic and Smith Street tattoos that no member of the proletariat could afford while drinking bobo beer at Saint Vitus.

24 **Serve themselves:** The author continues to relentlessly draw attention to the onanistic nature of design theory, his interest in drawing attention to the masturbation of others shows no more sign of abating than his criticism of death metal production does.

41 For design, by nature, is servitude's trade,
Its client's will is where decisions are made.
They say they serve users with justice in mind,
Yet the paycheck ensures whose goals are aligned.

45 'The best design is now just design,' they claim,
But justice undefined makes their virtue a game.
The roots of their morals, they dare not discuss,
And their own motives remain deeply sus."

49 I stared at the robed figures, faces pale, blank,
A voice called to me, but quickly it sank,
"Come, join, participate!" it urged in my ear,
Voice turned to noise, the end I could not hear.

53 Problematizing, their words so worn,
But in silent agreement, they were all sworn.
In perfect consent, they stumbled in line,
Marching together, as if by design.

57 Virgil looked down, contempt in his tone,
"They craft poetic projects, for themselves alone.
Designing the useless, with no thought of needs,
They profess and critique, while purpose bleeds.

---

46 **Justice:** The author mentions justice in three of the last four lines is obviously a debasement of the sad state Metallica found itself in after the aforementioned death of Cliff Burton, when they were forced to release an album almost entirely devoid of bass guitar after Scandavia rightfully took their bassist from them. The title *And Justice for All...* can only serve as an acknowledgement of the justice of their own predicament and foreshadowed the grim fate metal was to meet in the 90s when the only mainstream metal acts were Pantera and some nü metal bands whose names I cannot bring myself to mention.

48 **Sus:** Sus is a word often used by children on the internet to mean suspect in an especially pejorative manner, placing such a word in the mouth of a character named after an ancient reaffirms Otto's unshakable belief in the relevance of the classics in today's dark times.

57 **Virgil:** Virgil is the name of the character Ed Harris plays in James Cameron's classic film *The Abyss*, yet he also played Rear Admiral Chester "Hammer" Cain in 2022's *Top Gun: Maverick*. Hammer is Maverick's superior and the hard anvil on which his character is refined. The film is more proof that Hollywood takes recycling seriously and has a firm commitment to what it sees as its own classical tradition.

61 Design could rid the world of frictions and pain,
But they hide who profits, who reaps the gain.
They side with the outcast, the refugee's plight,
But flash their visas as their jets take height.

65 They see themselves as rebels, daring and bold,
While tied to markets they claim to scold.
These designers feign the trodden's view,
Preaching 'critical' as they the poorest screw.

69 A new elite distinction, a polished guise,
Signaling peers with knowing eyes.
While writing their paycheck in subversion's name,
They rise through the ranks in their subtle game.

73 Their virtues are veils, their justice a guise,
Their path is a circle of self-righteous lies.
On they march, in their gilded charade,
Never changing the system their hands have made."

77 A pang of guilt tore deeply through my chest,
My reservoir of bitter tears would not rest.
I was also among these proud, lofty souls,
But now felt shame for what had claimed our roles.

81 Virgil sighed, his gaze filled with disdain,
And we left the cloaked figures to their endless chain.
Downward we ventured, the path growing dark,
Leaving their chants to fade to a spark.

---

78 **Reservoir of tears:** As a reader one must appreciate how the author points to Dante's poetics of weeping and especially the *Cocytus,* or "the reservoir of tears," the frozen lake in the ninth circle of Hell where those guilty of treachery are frozen in ice and thus unable to weep or petition God for forgiveness. The continued references to Metallica, in this case *Ride the Lightning's* "Trapped under Ice," serve the same function that Creed did earlier in the text, possibly showing that the text is moving backward in time as the references grow older yet not tired.

CANTO
IX

Canto: Machiavell chose to put the body of the text of *The Prince* in the vernacular but put the chapter titles in latin, the language of both the ancients and the church, in order to give his text the majesty of his opponent and his heroes. Otto has repeated the same trick - Canto is both a Latin word and an Italian word - and his titles should be seen as both a statement about the degree to which the current orthodoxy has cemented itself in design theory and a desire to look to the past as a way forward the way that Machievelli did.

1   Amidst the cliffs, we found a shadowed glen,
    Where cries of anguish filled the air again.
    The ground was strewn with pebbles sharp and gray,
    Where wrestling figures in writhing fight lay.

5   Around their bodies, massive serpents coiled,
    Their self-esteem by brute force now despoiled.
    The snakes coiled tightly, crushing bone and pride,
    While screams of torment echoed far and wide.

9   Wails of pain rang out, a mournful song,
    As reality proved unyielding, fierce, and strong.
    Virgil observed and jeered, with mocking tone,
    "Behold the fools by their own hubris thrown.

13 See their pain and struggle, hear them whine,
    Now ensnared by the snakes of divine.
    They thought the world like PowerPoint slides,
    But now crushed by truths their art belies.

17 Social change, they said, was theirs to tame,
    A reality they could mold in their own name.
    Workshops, interventions, lofty abstractions—
    But not trusting the people's reactions.

[5] **Serpents coiled:** The repeated mention of coiled snakes is a clear reference to Slayer's "Spirit in Black" on *Seasons in the Abyss*, where the lord of the underworld repeatedly orders his serpents to unwind their coils and the denizens of hell discover their life was not what they thought it to be. The designers in this hell are in a far worse situation where they are literally crushed by their foolishness without coming to understand the falsity of their position, perhaps this very text will dissolve their perplexity and uncoil the serpents wrapped around so many of Otto's likely readership.

[14] **Snakes of the divine:** This is only one word different from the title track on High On Fire's *Snakes for the Divine*, a prime example of excellent songwriting and stellar musicianship triumphing over poor production, and this particular allusion expands Otto's criticism of contemporary metal production beyond the death metal world while providing design a glimmer of hope.

²¹ Relations, they claimed, was theirs to mold,
A sculpture shaped by intellects so bold.
But see them now, entangled, bound, and torn,
By truths of life they ignored with scorn.

²⁵ In the people's name, they devised their schemes,
Social Ponzis disguised as word morphemes.
Seeing people's lives as sculptures of clay,
Believing the world could be changed their way.

²⁹ Design, they said, transcends politics' strife,
Yet now they wrestle for a grip on life.
No skill to anchor, no plan to ignite,
Their visions strangled in this endless fight.

³³ They made shambles of their noble trade,
And now they're powerless, their ideals waylaid.
For when all's a designer, and all's a design,
No hands remain to draw the chalk circle line."

³⁷ I saw one wrestler, his body in strife,
Skin torn and bleeding, struggling for life.
Around his neck a serpent coiled thick,
He wheezed, "Social acupuncture is the trick."

---

²² **A sculpture shaped by intellects:** The designer's mistaken belief that they can use craft to shape social relations is in sharp distinction to the way the Greeks understood craft. Heidegger provides us with perhaps the clearest statement about Aristotle's understanding of craft in his lecture class on Plato's *Sophist*, which was attended by future journalist Hannah Arendt. Heidegger examines the five means the soul has of manifesting truth, which include craft or τέχνη. Τέχνη is the process by which the έργων comes into being through the work of the craftsman, who must have the look, εἶδος, of the finished product in mind before they can begin making and that the maker discloses the potential in the material to himself in the process. Otto's rejection of the scope of design embodied by those he puts in this corner of hell is clearly rooted in a similar understanding of the role of craft, one that affirms its central role in human life if denying it some of the grandi- osity afforded to it by his contemporaries. See Martin Heidegger *Plato's Sophist* pgs. 28-33.

²⁹ **Design:** If Otto was really interested in Heidegger he would have taken one of the many opportunities to take the pressure off his rhyme scheme by pairing dasein with design, so perhaps be weary of the violence of my previous comment.

³⁵ **All's a designer, and all's a design:** Otto doesn't even allow those cast into this part of hell the full seven stages of life Shakespeare identifies in the speech from *As You Like It* Otto is paraphrasing, these designers cannot even draw a chalk outline around the hollowness of their life let alone live anything that resembles a full life.

³⁷ **Wrestler:** The author brings to mind Mickey Rourke's hopelessly mangled face in Darren Aranofsky's 2008 film *The Wrestler*, a clear warning about the dangers of trying to apply design where it does not belong.

41 The wrestler fought on, with every ounce spent,
The serpent constricting, his body all bent.
I heard the ribs crack, like dry twigs in the breeze,
As he struggled and writhed, desperate to appease.

45 His strength was draining, the battle unkind,
As the serpent's grip tightened, no mercy to find.
Staying with the trouble, til the last breath,
I looked to Virgil, to the sound of death.

49 "Change Agents hoped the people could be led,
By artistic schemes and slogans softly said.
Their entanglement needs a crafty hand,
But concerted action they do not understand.

53 Interventions and their social reform,
Was quickly adrift in the civic storm.
No praxis, no authority, or guide,
Their visions splintered as the people cried.

57 Unruly souls, they could not reconcile,
Their plans undone by people's trial.
For people's loyalties demand their way,
And power shifts like shadows in the day.

61 They wrestle now with serpents in despair,
Grand peace crushed by forces unaware.
The world they sought to change resists their touch,
People's unruliness proving them too much."

46 **No mercy to find:** The serpent is following the
admonishment in the title of Slayer's 1983 debut
Show No Mercy.

⁶⁵ Virgil sighed deeply, "They shall not prevail,
For leadership, they lack; their efforts fail.
Reality's weight has crushed their flimsy art,
No cunning plan, no strategy, no heart."

⁶⁹ "This reality," Virgil scoffed, "won't yield to charm,
It bites and twists, it lashes out with harm.
These designers find the task too great to bear,
The civic realm's a maze, and they're ensnared.

⁷³ Their hopes of crafting unity from dust,
Collapse beneath the weight of human lust.
For power's not a game of mere design,
It's blood and toil, and hearts that intertwine."

⁷⁷ I watched them struggle, tangled in their fate,
Their ideas of design shattered in this state.
And as we turned, their groans began to fade,
The hell of other people left their hopes betrayed.

⁸¹ We walked away from their struggles dire and grim,
Their chances fleeting, their prospects ever slim.
Reality's serpents held them in their place,
And we walked on, as anguish etched my face.

---

⁷⁰ **Reality.. Bites:** Once again Virgil reminds us of the 1994 film, is Otto beginning to use the insipid mid 90's alternative rock found on its soundtrack the way he used Creed and Metallica earlier in the text?

⁷⁶ **Blood and toil:** The author's reference to Churchill's famous speeches is not only a hint to the enduring legacy of NWOBHM, but emphasizes how Strauss considered him an "indomitable and magnanimous statesman" and that Churchill reminds us to "seeing things as they are, [...] and therefore never to mistake mediocrity, however brilliant, for true greatness. In our age this duty demands of us in the first place that we liberate ourselves from the supposition that value statements cannot be factual statements." As bleak as this part of the text is, the reference to Maiden and their unrivalled ability to put out strong album after strong album over decade after decade provides a glimmer of hope for those who are trying to combine artistic integrity with obscene wealth. Quoted text is from remarks made by Strauss upon hearing of Churchill's death while teaching at the University of Chicago.

CANTO
X

Canto X: Machievelli wrote many books but only *The Prince* and *Discourses on Livy* claim to express all of Machievelli's knowledge of the world, given that Otto has put the entirety of the design world in hell the reader is right to ask which comprehensive statement of knowledge they should bring to bear on this extensive condemnation of un-knowledge. The reader simply needs to turn to the number of Cantos for their answer, Otto thinks little enough of his contemporaries that their entire world can be cast into hell in twenty fewer cantos than Dante needed and only half the number of chapters Macheivelli needed to use in *The Prince*. Machievelli traces his brevity to the Prince's need to absorb all of Macheivelli's knowledge of the world quickly: "No greater gift could be made by me than to give you the capacity to be able to understand in a very short time all that I have learned and understood in so many years and with so many hardships and dangers for myself. I have not ornamented this work, nor filled it with fulsome phrases nor with pompous or superfluous ornament whatever." The undeniability of Otto and Nicolio's common intent should put to bed any misgivings the reader may have about the necessity of my own commentary. Economy may not be the only factor driving Otto's decision to focus on *The Prince* and not *The Discourses,* the latter is an undeniably more difficult book and Otto may be meeting his audience on it's own terms. The quote is from the dedicatory letter of *The Prince.*

The number of cantos invites the reader to investigate whether Otto has put a wolf *(The Prince)* in sheep's clothing *(The Divine Comedy)* from Machievelli and not Dante. Does each of these 13 cantos correspond to two chapters of *The Prince?* If they do do so in a straightforward way this 10th canto would correspond to Machieavelli's 19th and 20th chapters, the latter of which clearly warns the prince against maintaining a fortress. Otto makes no such admonition in his text, likely because the positions held by those he condemns are not strong enough to be mistaken for a molehill let alone a fortress and his text is committed to the principles of economy mentioned in the previous footnote.

1   The path grew steeper, the way full of dread,
     A dark gorge before us, where shadows spread.
     We moved on slowly, my heart wrecked with pain,
     Virgil led us deeper, where blood does reign.

5   Along the valley stretched a woeful band,
     Their bodies torn by some unseen command.
     Flesh was flayed, their blood soaked every stone,
     With hanging entrails dragging, their pain alone.

9   Virgil halted, gazing at their plight,
     "Behold these souls who sought their private right.
     Their suffering born of a twisted quest,
     To make their selves the truth, above the rest.

13   Their ego is Omphalos' exalted seat,
     And now their inner shredding is complete.
     They sought their worth in self-examined pain,
     And carved their hearts to find their truth in vain."

17   Cut open, bowles hanging, their inners apart,
     We saw them vivisected, bleeding from the start.
     Their bodies writhe, belly and guts now hollow,
     Organs that make shit from what we swallow.

---

4 **Blood does reign:** Yet another reference to Slayer's genre defining 1986 record *Reign in Blood*. Does the paucity of references to contemporary metal reflect a justifiably harsh judgment of the current scene, a commitment to textual economy, or a dim judgement of the cultural literacy of the likely reader? Or does it say something about his confidence in my ability to spot more obscure metal references, a fear he must have spent enough time with me both at Saint Vitus and in my home to know is unfounded?

7 **Flesh was flayed:** The author continues to hone in on the classics by inserting yet another Slayer reference, in this case making mention of "Piece by Piece," the second song on Slayers groundbreaking 1986 album *Reign in Blood*. Indeed the design theorists in this part of hell

must pass the Angel of Death and the meaning of pain before reaching the Altar of Sacrifice, the table of hell.

9 **Gazing etc:** One has to read Virgil against Leo Strauss' famous dictum in the lecture class reprinted as *On Plato's Symposium;* "But what is the core of the political? Men killing men on the largest scale in broad daylight and with the greatest serenity." Despite the words that Otto has put in the mouth of his character Virgil make no mistake - it is Otto himself serenely dispatching his colleagues to hell in the bright sunshine of his ivory tower.

13 **Omphalos:** The reader hardly needs me to tell him this is an older name for the Delphic Oracle, but perhaps I could remind them that Joyce makes repeated use of the word in *Ulysses?*

21 "They craft their selves with antiauthority,
Yet bind their souls in the market's decree.
From situatedness, they rise anew, deceived,
Their world revolves around what they've conceived.

25 They twist their lives to match their cries of woe,
Demanding their ordeals all world must know.
They say self-knowledge means wisdom firm,
Yet it stays a contradiction in term.

29 Now trapped within their endless inward gaze,
They lost the light of any common ways.
For every claim they make of deeper hurt,
Leaves them more powerless, ground to dirt.

33 Identity, their inner citadel as well as chain,
Denounces strength to everlasting pain.
They've lost the art of building common cause,
For every grievance breeds its separate laws."

37 I saw the suckers stumble on the bones,
slipping in blood with agonizing groans.
Then Virgil pointed, his voice stern and clear,
and spoke once more for all the damned to hear.

41 "Rules they revile, as shackles to their pride,
Yet victimhood now is their trusted guide.
Their freedom stands on critical disdain,
While careers bloom in market-traded pain.

---

35 **Art of building:** The constant references to Slayer's *Reign in Blood* force the reader to recall Clint Eastwood's role in 1986's *Heartbreak Ridge*, where his character, Marine Sgt. Thomas Highway, quips "The only thing you could build is a good case of hemorrhoids."

40 **And spoke once again for all the dammed to hear:** Yet again Otto has his character enlighten the damned about the source of their condition, and the reader has to wonder why he continues to put the harsher judgments in his character's mouth and not in the mouth of the character that bears his own name. Does he think little enough of his contemporaries to believe his rouse will work?

Or is it meant to underscore the depth of his contempt to the careful reader who will not be thrown off by such simple rhetorical tricks?

43 **Freedom stands:** Yet again the author ridicules Metallica's *Ride the Lightning*, which takes its title from a passage in Stephen King's 1978 novel *The Stand*, indicating that the sad tropes of the album's D minor key certainly deserve the electric chair. Anthrax plays a more appropriate homage to King's novel on their 1987 *Among The Living*. Otto's continual references to Metallica's peers drives home the true injustice of the way the financial circumstances of the so called "Big Four" played out.

⁴⁵ Authenticity, a banner they unfurl,
Protects them from the normative whirl.
While others fall to algorithms' might,
They stake their claim in marginal delight."

⁴⁹ A man slipped on his guts, a grotesque display,
As the words bled out in a tortured array.
"The personal is political," his voice croaked bloody,
A mantra of pain, raw and muddy.

⁵³ "The narcissist clings to their fragile worth,"
Virgil spoke, to the man's ruptured girth.
"In every grievance, they find their refrain,
Immolation serves to ease their pain.

⁵⁷ As the world burns and others suffer deep,
They focus solely on their wounds to keep.
Creation once profound now feels so small,
But their egos thrive, above it all."

⁶¹ Virgil sighed, his voice both soft and grim,
"Their suffering springs from the depths within.
For as they turn their gaze to only me,
They find no strength in shared humanity.

⁶⁵ This is cannibalizing design, a savage rite,
They feast on grief and claim their inner plight.
Each tear they shed demands the world to see,
Yet scorns the hands that build solidarity.

---

⁶² **Depths within:** Again the author makes a reference to the fifth track on Mgła's seminal *Exercises in Futility* with its damning critique of critical theory, where "the guilt, the fear, the woe and the betrayal" are not systemic traits of social oppression, but "come from within," that is, from the acculturation of taste, dooming false metal to the hell of self-absorbed teen angst.

⁶³ **Gaze to only me:** Another damning critique of hipster shoe-gaze "black metal" such as Alcest with their simplistic adoption of fuzzy riffs stolen from early Sonic Youth and a worthwhile if sometimes cloying strain of English guitar rock. Could there be a bigger triumph of bad design than the bright pink cover of Deafheaven's *Sunbather*, which allowed an imitation of an imitation to be sold to a mainstream audience?

⁶⁵ **Cannibalizing:** Making reference to Cannibal Corpse highlights the necrophilic tendencies exhibited by commercially successful death metal that has long ago lost any relevance to the scene despite the technical proficiency shown on many of their newer records.

⁶⁹ They seek no kinship, only wounds to bare,
To weave a tale of torment, raw and rare.
Attacking bonds that might their pain assuage,
They lock themselves within a bleeding cage.

⁷³ Enclosed, the Sicilian bull becomes their tomb,
A statue forged by their self-fashioned gloom.
Their cries rise up, yet none will heed their song,
For unity's the path they've deemed all wrong."

⁷⁷ I felt a pang of guilt and gazed upon my toil,
how I had let my pain cause others' dreams to spoil.
My tears fell swiftly, and my body shook with woe,
for the harm I'd done by the weight I'd come to know.

⁸¹ With heavy heart, I turned to walk away,
While cries of pain pursued our way.
Behind, they staggered, bound in grief's embrace,
Forever seeking peace they'd not replace.

---

⁷⁰ **Weave a tale:** The author juxtaposes Wittgenstein's comments on dismembering action in favor of empty jargon in *On Certainty* (OC402) and the opening lines of Mgla's 2015 *Exercises in Futility;* "The great truth is that there isn't one, And it only gets worse, Since that conclusion."

⁷⁴ **A statue:** Citing Mgla screaming "Hollow" so quickly after the previous reference confirms the note above. I can attest that the repeated references to Mgla can be explained in accordance with William of Occam's famous dictum: Otto really, really likes them.

CANTO
XI

¹ Through shadowed valleys, we stumbled on,
To a cavernous space where light was gone.
Shadows flickered on blood-soaked stone,
Limbs dismembered, yet minds alone.

⁵ Arms and legs severed, yet restless still,
Hands kept writing verses, as if by will.
Heads mumbled fragments, fingers twitched,
Scrawling citations as though bewitched.

⁹ Eyes still reading, a head softly spoke,
Quoting wisdoms in a chopped-up croak.
Shattered limbs, they moved through strife,
A dance macabre, a mockery of life

¹³ On a ledge, a tall figure stood,
Its severed head held firm as wood.
The mouth spoke verses, a torrent of sound,
Echoes of texts that once were profound.

¹⁷ I heard some words in language unknown,
And others too complex to grasp or own.
Yet bodies around me nodded slow,
As if they understood what none could know.

---

³ **Shadows, etc:** *The Shadows* are the regicidal organization that sends Gradus to kill King Charles the Beloved, but Otto is not thinking of John Shade as much as the continuous fratricide amongst academic doppelgangers, each one less interesting than the other, yet all with equally inflated self worth. The repeated use of the word Shadow points the reader to Dostoevsky's second novel, 1846's *Dvoynik ("The Double")*, about a struggling low-level bureaucrat on the verge of insanity encountering his double, only to be dragged off to an asylum.

¹² **Dance macabre:** The author makes light of the infamous incident where Messiah Marcolin, singer of the epic doom-metal band Candlemass, pounded himself through the stage in a forceful display of the dangers of combining truly heavy riffs, lager, and a lack of exercise.

¹² **Dance macabre:** *Dance Macabre* is the name of Stephen King's 1981 treatise on horror writing that he drafted during a short lived stint as an academic, which is an odd choice at first blush. Why make mention of one of King's two or three worst books when he could allude to the Dark Tower saga or any number of classics? Otto is,

put simply, boasting: as you can see his short time as a poet has been much more successful than King's time as an academic was, and this is the one time his bravado shows through his repeated insistence that he shares some of the blame for the state of design theory.

¹⁶ **Echoes of texts that were once profound:** Otto has chosen to put his poem in iambic pentameter, a meter that goes back as far as Homer, and this seems like a natural choice at first. Aristotle notes in the fourth section of the Poetics that the meter shares its name with the Greek word for mockery, ἰαμβίζειν, because it was it's initial use, although he is quick to point out that it was quickly adopted by Homer and others who wanted to write more serious texts. So far so good, right? Otto has chose to write his ancient poem in a meter though to be both mocking and serious by the ancients. ὥστε τρεῖς ἂν εἶεν φιλοσοφίαι θεωρητικαί, μαθηματική, φυσική, θεολογική (οὐ γὰρ ἄδηλον ὅτι εἴ που τὸ θεῖον ὑπάρχει, ἐν τῇ τοιαύτῃ φύσει ὑπάρχει), καὶ τὴν τιμιωτάτην δεῖ περὶ τὸ τιμιώτατον γένος εἶναι. 1026(a)

²¹ Severed hands wrote with careful grace,
As if each word held meaning in its place.
They seemed to find the deepest truth in the air,
While I was lost, confused, and unaware.

²⁵ "Behold," said Virgil, with weary throat,
"These are the thinkers who bleed for a quote.
For them, words alone are the ultimate creed,
No action, no change, just endless screed."

²⁹ "Hear these preachers of morality,"
Scorned Virgil, in sordid brutality.
"Reciting the dead, their wisdom borrowed,
From lives unlived, these thoughts are hollowed.

³³ They quote and cite with fervent zeal,
Of unknown pleasures, their truths unreal.
Their dogmas make the world grow small,
With nudged intolerance as advice for all."

³⁷ I sobbed at the sight, agony in my chest,
"Yes," said Virgil, "their morals professed,
Are stitched from texts, they endlessly quote,
No new idea, at best a footnote."

²² **Careful grace:** Strauss is full of passages on the importance of taking mistakes made by a great author seriously. See, e.g., this passage from *Thoughts on Machievelli* "Machievelli's work if rich in manifest blunders of various kinds... It is a rule of common prudence to "believe" that all these blunders are intentional and in each case to raise the question as to what the blunder might be meant to signify."

³¹ **Wisdom borrowed:** The criticism of false black metal continues, with another swipe at shoegaze inspired black metal and the insipid influence of Godspeed You! Black Emperor. As Otto would say "Just think of Agalloch's *The Mantle,* and weep."

³⁴ **Truths unreal:** These scholars are much like the Exciter mentioned on the first track of Judas Priest's 1978 album *Stained Class.* As mentioned above Otto opened the text by quoting the songs from this album in reverse order, as if he was playing the album backwards to the reader, but here he arrives at what would be the end of the album if you were playing it backwards without quoting "Better by you, Better than me." This confirms that he means the reader no harm, and while he may be willing to invoke the spectre of evil the text is ultimately altruistic. Rob Halford mentioned that playing Exciter backwards makes him appear to sing "I asked her for a peppermint, I asked her to get one" during their trial, and while Otto is offering the reader something more substantial than candy he hardly needs to tell those who are already in hell to kill themselves on his behalf and may even be offering them some hope, or at least a small amount of sustenance.

⁴⁰ **At best a footnote:** The careful reader will notice that the criticism of footnotes is restricted to academic texts and Otto is not criticizing the many excellent literary uses of footnotes in books like Nabokov's *Pale Fire,* Nichelson Baker's *Mezzanine,* David Foster Wallace's *Infinite Jest* and this text's many other forbears. I must take this space to insist that unlike the previously mentioned examples I am a real person who is not a ghost or a drug addict, and I do not appear elsewhere in the text. It is also true that Otto and I have been neighbors (and friends) for many years.

⁴¹ "They address the profound," Virgil sneered,
"Yet change is absent, as we have feared.
Their peers applaud their cited fame,
But a world dismembered remains the same.

⁴⁵ Listen closely, they speak of care,
They fight the system with wordy air.
Raising 'awareness,' they loudly claim,
Yet all they care for is their own name.

⁴⁹ They count their worth in citations tall,
A hollow metric, their gospel's call.
'Impact,' they say, but it's all pretend,
It's all cut n' paste ideology with no end."

⁵³ A mouth spoke of "web of science" and numbers bought,
And "h-index" and how not to get caught.
But the voice was distant, dull, and unclear,
Echoing words that I could hardly hear.

⁵⁷ "These bleeding buggers," Virgil sneered in disgust,
"They butcher each author, betraying all trust.
Mutilating every work for selfish success,
Taking only what serves their own emptiness."

⁶¹ The dissected members twitched on the cold, dark ground,
Movements grotesque, to the murmuring sound.
Severed heads lectured in fragmented speech,
Endless recitals as if the dead to teach.

---

⁴³ **Cited fame:** These two words completely erase any worry I may have about who this portion of the text is aimed at.

⁴⁸ **Raising 'awareness' etc:** This section must be read against Leo Strauss' *Liberalism Ancient and Modern*, where Strauss posits that "Only a great fool would call the new political science diabolic: it has no attributes peculiar to fallen angels. It is not even Machiavellian, for Machiavelli's teaching was graceful, subtle, and colorful. Nor is it Neronian. Nevertheless one may say of it that it fiddles while Rome burns. It is excused by two facts: it does not know that it fiddles, and it does not know that Rome burns." Otto's text serves as a poignant reminder that design theory is indeed burning, and his constant metal references can be seen as an insistent reminder that academic endeavors can be accompanied by something far better than folk music.

⁵⁷ **Bleeding buggers:** This is most likely a typo, the author clearly means burghers.

⁶⁴ **Severed heads ... dead to teach:** A clear reference to Cattle Decapitation's 2019 opus *Death Atlas*, with its prescient song "Bring back the plague," which allowed them to post the phrase "Bring Back the Plague Tour cancelled by Actual Human Plague" or something similar on social media. Coincidentally Cattle Decapitation was the last band both Otto and I saw before the pandemic.

65 Seeking wisdom to see through the haze,
With tearful eyes, I saw Virgil's gaze.
Guiding me through this bloodstained fear,
He spoke without haste, steady and clear.

69 "Text upon text, such butchered tide,
With no plans for actions left inside.
Here reality is but text and a map,
But, come on, that's bullshit, such piece of crap."

73 I wept for the waste, the endless grind,
Bleeding, butchered, meaning left behind.
Virgil sighed, "These horrors you see
Are just the start; worse yet will be."

77 Darkness spun in chaos, a blur of dismay,
How had I become one of these, led astray?
I fell to my knees, consumed by the pain,
Tore at my flesh—how was I just the same?

81 I trembled, cried, my hope undone,
"What horror worse could still become?"
Virgil whispered, leading me near,
"The darkest depths still wait us here."

72 **Piece of crap:** The author borrows a turn of phrase from his better known contemporary Ralf Wronsov.

73 **Endless grind:** A cheap shot at grindcore bands, who can seldom play at speed for more than thirty seconds at a time in a live setting or hold the listener's interest for much longer on a record. Otto's scholarly duties prevented him from seeing any of the three recent Gridlink performances given during the last days of Saint Vitus, which would have surely ripped the scales off his eyes, softening his critique.

CANTO
XII

¹ Deep where nothing shines, the air grew stark,
The wind howled bitter, a subzero spark.
The ground beneath, a frozen slate,
A lake of ice bore a dreadful fate.

⁵ Bodies entombed in the crystal floor,
Contorted forms, trapped evermore.
Beneath icy surface, bodies lay still,
Twisted in torment, frozen without will.

⁹ Heads poked through with frost-bitten stares,
Silent witnesses to their icy affairs.
Blue lips whispered frozen negation,
Icicles clung to this frosted sedation.

¹³ "Witness," said Virgil, his voice severe,
"We've reached the bottom, the end is near.
So cool these thinkers, their life frozen clear,
Refusing action, and paralyzed by fear.

¹⁷ Virgil pointed, now his voice like stone,
"Here lie passive judges, chilled to the bone.
Their lives were spent in critical gaze,
But their frozen hearts could spark no blaze.

---

² **Zero:** Otto has spent most of his life confused by the way that Black Sabbath could put a shortened version of "Zero the Hero" on the B-side on the 1983 "Trashed" single, which betrays a charming but odd understanding of the way that vinyl works. But he would like you to know that if you are a true believer you can still find that beautiful piece of vinyl on Discogs for around 10 bucks.

¹¹ **Blue lips:** The author is showing off his medical knowledge, Cyanosis is indicative of a lack of oxygen in the blood, only in this case the condition is brought on by the stagnant condition of contemporary design theory and not having reached exalted heights or rarified air.

¹³ **Virgil:** Virgil is the name of the character Ed Harris plays in James Cameron's classic film *The Abyss*, yet in 1998's *The Truman Show*, Harris plays Christof, the director of the televised universe that traps Truman in a completely artificial reality designed to keep him from understanding how larger forces profit from the banality of his quotidian life. The 1998 film is a sanitized version of Philip K Dick's 1959 novel *Time Out of Joint*, where a character is forced to live in a similarly artificial world because he cannot conscience his ability to predict where the lunar rebels, with whom the main character rightfully sympathies with, will aim their next nuclear strikes. Otto's previous allusions to Philip K Dick prevent the reader from adopting the more anodyne interpretation and cement the lack of irony in Otto's own admissions of complicity in the current state of academic design.

²⁰ **Could spark no blaze:** The allusion to Darkthrone's iconic second album is likely intended to counterbalance the description of the frozen state of these particular residents of hell, which veers dangerously close to the approving language bands like Immortal use to describe their riffage, by reminding us that these frigid scholars are incapable of inspiring any kind of fire, whether it be in loins or a Scandinavian church in the 90s. "See the opening of Nabokov's *Lolita*.

²¹ Cynics of Babel, they tear down with disdain,
   Safe behind words, they avoid the strain.
   The world's a discourse, a tale of speech,
   But action itself is beyond their reach.

²⁵ Fear kept them still, in judgment they froze,
   Afraid to act, they rejected the throes.
   To risk, to struggle, to build and create—
   They chose to passively speculate."

²⁹ I shivered as my feet grew numb with biting chill,
   yet feared to glance below, my heart frigid still.
   I dreaded my reflection would meet my eyes,
   but Virgil spoke again beneath the frozen skies.

³³ "These are cold cynics, who freeze to displace,
   Discarding the world, with judgment's disgrace.
   A disaster they are, the disease of design,
   Servants of all Dis, with hearts cold and blind.

³⁷ Passivity binds them, theory is their snare,
   Their biting inertia, a prison laid bare.
   Each verdict they cast was a chilling decree,
   That now locks them here in eternity."

⁴¹ Hopelessly I shivered in the biting cold,
   Bending down closer, my courage now bold.
   There, stuck deep in ice, an author's glare,
   Cold, judgmental eyes that pierced the air.

---

33 **Cynic:** An approving reference to the band Cynic, who were able to leverage their time with Chuck Schuldinger in Death to create an unlikely blend of technical death metal and jazz that no true metalhead can be, well, cynical enough to deny despite the use of vocoders. The enormity of this achievement cannot be understated.

33 **Cynic:** Otto's near constant references to music provide yet more evidence that his poem should be read as a tragedy, Aristotle gives music as one of the elements of tragedy in section 6 of his *Poetics. καὶ εἴπερ ἔστι τις τοιαύτη φύσις ἐν τοῖς οὖσιν, ἐνταῦθ᾽ ἂν εἴη που καὶ τὸ θεῖον, καὶ αὕτη ἂν εἴη πρώτη καὶ κυριωτάτη ἀρχή.* 1064(a)

43 **Stuck under ice:** Even the most hopelessly culturally illiterate reader will know that this is a reference to Metallica's "Trapped Under Ice" by this point.

⁴⁵ I felt the loathing in those frozen eyes,
Speechless contempt, no words, no disguise.
I recoiled from the gaze, my heart filled with dread,
A solid silence, a scolding left unsaid.

⁴⁹ Virgil stood quiet, his face filled with grief,
His eyes spoke of sorrow, of no relief.
He spoke with a bitterness, sharp as a knife,
"See the cowardness of a cynic life."

⁵³ "They cry, 'We've changed the discourse, you see!'
But passive decrees are empty debris.
In this age, where language inflates and decays,
Their speech means nothing, their inertia betrays.

⁵⁷ Science denied, yet jargon profound,
Speech without meaning, a tiring sound.
Frozen in powerlessness, they sit and blame,
Casting contempt, yet refusing the shame.

⁶¹ They call for empathy, yet judge with ease,
Incompatible forces meant to please.
This lake now holds their frozen scorn,
Each judgment made, a life forlorn."

⁶⁵ I saw their faces, hard and cold,
Eyes that judged but never were bold.
Their mouths, still frozen, formed silent jeers,
While their souls succumbed to their sissy fears.

---

⁴⁶ **No disguise:** An unmistakable reference to the twin cultural calamities of 1983: Kiss' unmasking at the start of the unfortunate "Lick it up" era at the same time that Derrida became *directeur d'études* at the École des Hautes Études en Sciences Sociales in Paris.

⁵⁴ **Empty debris:** The author's relentless exposure of the damage that Metallica did to their "souls" continues with a brief mention of their absolute wreckage after Jason Newstead of Flotsam and Jetsam was the best they could do after they got their just desserts for daring to bring their false metal to Scandinavia. Fuck around and find out, as the kids say.

⁶⁶ **Judge... Bold:** Otto manages to work the names of two of the most important NYHC bands of the eighties into just ten syllables.

⁶⁸ **Sissy fears:** The unceasing depiction on the suffering of the designers that Otto has confined to hell reminds the reader that one of the requirements of a tragedy given by Aristotle in section eleven of the *Poetics* is that the suffering of the characters be displayed. Otto hardly displays anything other than suffering in his poem, which makes it something more than a tragedy without ever veering into melodrama. τὸ γὰρ δεκτικὸν τοῦ νοητοῦ καὶ τῆς οὐσίας νοῦς, ἐνεργεῖ δὲ ἔχων, ὥστ´ ἐκείνου μᾶλλον τοῦτο ὃ δοκεῖ ὁ νοῦς θεῖον ἔχειν, καὶ ἡ θεωρία τὸ ἥδιστον καὶ ἄριστον. 1072(b)

69 "Passivity's weight is heavier still,"
Said Virgil, "than the mightiest will.
For in doing nothing, they sealed their fate,
Forever locked in this icy state."

73 Tears streamed down but froze on my cheek,
Their bitter frost made me weak.
"What doom for design, to end like this!"
But Virgil replied, "This is the truth's abyss."

77 "Come," he beckoned, his pace unrelenting,
"This is but one of design's lamenting.
Ahead lies the final end to be told,
Follow, though the truth bites cold."

81 I shivered and staggered, the lake at my back,
Through the darkness, along the track.
The chills of judgment faded to gloom,
As we marched down design's sunken tomb.

---

79 **Final end:** Otto manages to remove any relief
the reader may feel at the imminent conclusion
of their trip to hell by mocking them with Marilyn
Manson's cover of The Doors' classic "The End,"
which was recorded for the 2020 television
adaptation of Stephen King's *The Stand*.

CANTO XIII

Canto XIII: As the poem comes to a close the reader can no longer afford to postpone the difficult question of how far Otto has been willing to follow Machievelli. Strauss clearly sets out Machievelli's project of recruiting an army who will free Italy from Christianity after his death, putting Machievelli in the position of a Moses who frees his people but does not live to see them to the promised land. That project is clearly stated in Strauss' chapter on the *Discoures* in *Thoughts on Machiavelli*, is Otto's will to live the reason that he continually draws the reader to the *Prince* and not the *Discourses?* Moses also appears in the *Prince* where he is one of four acquisitive princes that Machiavelli singles out for praise, all of whom are literary characters, even though Machiavelli is quick to say that Moses should not be discussed because he merely executed God's plan. Who is God and who is Moses here? Is the true Moses Otto's character Otto, who is executing his maker's plan? Is Otto acknowledging that the state of design theory is dire enough that he could not possibly live to see it through its current orthodoxy? Machieveli had to go to great lengths to show that Christianity is man made and has a natural lifetime, something that Otto is spared, but the task must seem nearly insurmountable. Does Otto believe that his slim book, not even as long as Mansfiled's translation of *The Prince,* is sufficient to recruit an army? Moses is an odd character in the Bible, God says that he is forced to provide him with his brother Aaron because of Moses' inability to speak eloquently, yet Moses delivers most of the well known speeches in that part of the Bible. Is this why Otto has Virgil do all the talking here? Aristotle's admonishment that the poet should not speak in his own voice is only aimed at epic poets. Am I Otto's Aaron? His text is hardly more eloquent than mine.

1   We walked across the lake, its ice so cold,
    And found a rock from which depths unfold.
    From there, we gazed upon the nethermost deep,
    Horror unseen where even death did sleep.

5   At the lowest point, where silence dwells,
    Virgil spoke softly, as deadened bells:
    "Here's the pit's nadir, where all paths converge,
    The gravity well of despair's bitter surge.

9   It is the heart of torment, the naught of design,
    Where frozen action and treachery align."
    In the icy lake, a giant did loom,
    Disruptor and traitor, presiding in gloom.

13 The ice stretched wide, deep frost within,
    And in its cold grasp the captor of sin.
    Three faces gnawed on their traitorous prey,
    Hellmouths, eternal, frozen in decay.

17 Virgil intoned, "Behold here, Dis Pater of design,
    Promethean dis-ign turned toxic in time.
    Dives, disruptor and root this dark call,
    Creation's ascent and its harrowing fall.

[11] **Icy lake:** Another sad reference to Celtic Frost's 1988 album *Cold Lake*, pointing to how there is no limit to the horrid punishment that befalls once groundbreaking artists turned into poseurs, a term that has remained among the most stinging in the English language since I was in high school.

[14] **Captor of sin:** Otto truly seems to have wholeheartedly adopted Slayer's vocabulary for describing hell, "Captor of Sin" is a song on their *Haunting The Chapel* EP that was a mainstay of their live set for many years. See *Decade of Aggression* for the definitive edition with better production. It's also slightly faster.

[16] **Three... Hellmouths:** Slayer's influence appears to have gone beyond language to the visual, consider Larry Carroll's defining cover art for Slayer's three most influential albums: *Reign In Blood*, *South Of Heaven*, and *Seasons In The Abyss*.

[17] **Dis:** Dis is the purported site of Merlin's orange crystal ball in Stephen King's *Dark Tower* series, Otto's telepathic ability to read the lesser minds of his contemporaries puts his in the position of both the mythical Merlin and the forces of the Dark Man in King's magnum opus.

[20] **Creation's ascent:** A clear reference to the early 80's German scene, particularly Teutonic thrash titans Kreator and their twin masterpieces *Endless Pain* and *Pleasure to Kill*.

21 One mouth chews the traitor of tradition,
   Scorned past lessons in reckless ambition.
   Another chews through solidarity's thread,
   Where bonds of the many were left for dead.

25 The third mouth grinds hope's betrayer to dust,
   Who promised the world, but broke its trust."
   I saw Dis weep tears mingled with blood,
   A dark lamentation freezing the flood.

29 "The fire of design that promised to heal,
   Burned through the bonds that made us feel.
   Now all is ice, a cold, empty fate,
   The heat-death of hope, the world of late."

33 Virgil's voice rose over the icy wind,
   "Here lies the depth where design rescinds,
   The end of the path, where all seems lost,
   Yet it is here you can begin to exhaust

37 The illusions of reason, the folly of pride,
   Are the truths that this sad crater will provide.
   For to this pit, no shortcut exists,
   You climb with the knowledge that struggle insists."

35 **The end of the path:** The state of the narrator and his guide at the end of their journey immediately brings to mind the condition that Gulliver finds himself in at the end of *Gulliver's Travels* - he has returned home from his time spent among the Houyhnhnms, a race of horses clearly modelled after the "ideal" society described in Plato's Republic, in a canoe made of human flesh blissfully unaware of how his time among his betters robbed him of his humanity. The character Otto has had the opposite experience - his time among his inferiors has made him aware of his own shortcomings but given him hope. Swift and Otto occupy a unique position in literary history - they are the only two satirical authors to completely destroy all of their predecessors, even if Otto only takes on those in his chosen field. Swift's achievement cannot be understated.

⁴¹ My failings exposed, cruel, bitter and cold,
A taste in my mouth, of desperation's hold.
Frozen tears burned sharp on my face,
As Virgil urged us to leave this place.

⁴⁵ Virgil turned with a glimmering eye,
And pointed, as to push away the sky.
"The journey itself has taught you seeing,
That despair is the furnace where doing is being.

⁴⁹ Each circle descended, each shadow we passed,
Has carved you a lesson meant to last.
The fears you have faced, the doubts endured,
Have forged an insight no comfort ensured.

⁴⁴ **Leave this place:** We can now confirm that Otto has chosen to confine the dramatic date of his poem to a single day, which Aristotle identifies as a hallmark of tragedy in section five of his *Poetics*. Otto's poem contains too many of the hallmarks of tragedy for it to be a coincidence. In addition to the use of meter and focus on suffering mentioned above Aristotle also says that a tragedy must include music, must include many recognitions, must inspire pity and fear in the audience, is most effective when it uses slightly odd language, and he even identifies and entire subgenre of tragedy set entirely in the underworld. I hardly need to reiterate how Otto's poem clearly meets so many of these criteria. Could Otto's entire project be said to be forcing the current state of design to recognize what and where it truly is, forcing the kind of tragic recognitions Oedipus suffers on nearly every scholar in his field? A positive answer to that question would bode well for Otto's regard for his peers, for a key part of Aristotle's definition of tragedy is a great man destroying himself, and he also requires the viewer to pity those who they see suffer just as much as the tragic poet is required to speak of humans who are better than those in the real world. Whether or not the reader finds this work tragic may well depend on whether or not Otto has robbed them of their ability to see themselves in their fellow scholars.

⁴⁷ **The journey itself has taught you seeing:** Virgil's use of a visual metaphor for knowledge reminds us that Otto has literally enacted the metaphor of the cave from Plato's *Republic*, and can now see the true form of things in the light of reason. Strauss offered at least two classes on that text and devoted a chapter in *The City and Man* to it, which the reader is invited to examine if he wants to see Strauss provide evidence of a "hidden teaching" he does not bother to state.

⁴⁸ **Doing is being:** This line reveals the true extent of Otto's ambition: With Heidegger's help we have already established that Aristotle understood craft as the process by which the maker's idea of the look of the finished work brought out the potential of the material, but what if Otto has dared to take things a step further and is bold enough to believe that craft puts the maker in the position of the prime mover, which is what Aristotle called his God in the *Metaphysics*. This would make a reader who has taken this poem's teacher to heart the prime maker, allowing them to access the divinity in both themselves and their materials. This makes the true ambition of Otto's work truly staggering, and allows him to pull off the same kind of trick that English departments were able to do in the 90s by using philosophical texts to redefine the boundaries of their discipline, only Otto has managed to do so without making use of the same French writers that have been kicking around academia since before he was an undergraduate.

⁵³ The disruptor's fall is the maker's ascent,
Through despair's embrace, your strength is lent.
Alchemy of soul, dissolve and reform,
Through trial and error, true work is born."

⁵⁷ Climbing on Dis, his limbs the stair,
Through twisted burrows of frozen air.
The world turned, the space rearranged,
A surreal staircase, endlessly strange.

⁶¹ Now ascending the dark, my fear in retreat,
Drawn to proportions more orderly, neat.
The present stood open, no barriers in sight,
The space of advent, the concrete to excite.

⁶⁵ "From abyss to workshop, the lesson is clear:
You must carry the wisdom you found here.
The virtue of silence, not spoken aloud,
But earned through descent, what shadows enshroud.

⁶⁹ For the emerald wisdom is born in the strife,
The labor of soul, the shaping of life.
You dissolved in the dark, reassembled anew,
Through chymical wedding your craft may grow true."

⁷³ At last, we stood where creation begins,
No lock to pick, no need to break in.
The workshop lay open, a space without end,
A forge of hope, where despair learns to bend.

---

⁵⁶ **True work is born:** This observation of Virgil marks the absolute nadir of the poem, the low point in the journey before the two companions can start their ascent. Here Otto once again uses Judas Priest lyrics as a touch stone, this time invoking the Halford's recent writing "Trial by Fire" that points back to the connections between their 1990 trial, "subliminal messaging," and esoteric writing; "Where I left my mark, When the system fell, You were in my grasp, Hid behind your veil." The reader recognizes how Halford, a born again Christian, uses the phrasing "behind your veil" to draw attention to John Shade's endeavors to look "beyond the veil" in Mrs. Z's poem "The Land Beyond the Veil," alluding to the afterlife and the presence of God in every act of creation.

⁶⁷ **Silence:** Virgil's silence is almost shocking given the amount of speaking Otto had him do throughout their journey. See Leo Strauss *Thoughts on Machiavelli:* "The silence of a wise man is always meaningful."

⁷⁵ **Space without end:** The space in the workshop has become an endless yet void of character, much as Martin Heidegger and Jacob Klein characterize the modern experience of space as nothing more than an empty grid that can be conquered, as enabled by the triumph of modern physics. See the first part of Heidegger's *What is a Thing?* and the last chapter of Klein's *Greek Mathematical Thought and the Origin of Algebra.*

⁷⁷ "Here lies design," Virgil softly said,
"Not beheld of Agon, but Irene instead.
Your path through depths, the struggle you faced,
Is the sagacity of Salomon no void can erase.

⁸¹ This gold is not the common gold,
The work a journey that cannot be told.
These tools are not the common tools,
A pilgrimage below educes your rules."

⁸⁵ "Now find your workbench," Virgil did say,
"The work's redemption must be found this way.
Through labor and learning, craft and care,
Abyss calls unto abyss to become repair."

⁸⁹ I touched the workbench, my hands met the wood,
The tools were known, as if they understood.
A beginner's mind, Occam's tools in my grasp,
The stars of our work, to hold and to clasp.

---

⁷⁷ **Virgil:** Virgil is the name of the character Ed Harris plays in James Cameron's classic film *The Abyss*, who knowingly descends to the bottom of the pit knowing that it will be a one-way trip, all without losing a sense of humor about himself in the face of death.

⁷⁹ **Path through depth:** The final mention of the depths in the cantos draws us back full circle to the sixth line of the first canto, where the inquisitive reader finds a clear reference to "At the Fathomless Depths," the ominous and solemn intro of Dissection's epic 1995 album *Storm of the Light's Bane*, which manages to seamlessly meld black and thrash metal in a way any craftsman would be proud of.

⁸⁸ **To become repair:** Virgil's departing words immediately bring Plato's *Protagoras* to mind. See 348c7-d5.

⁹⁰ **Understood:** The finishing four lines affirms that Otto, like Shade before him, now understands there is no need for the white fountain.

⁹⁰ **The tools were known:** Otto's repudiation of Heidegger's account of the hammer in *Being and Time,* and those who name books after it, is driven home yet again.

⁹¹ **Occam's tools:** The image of the razor manages to bind together quite a few of Otto's preoccupations: that of the blade master V in Alan Moore and David Lloyd's *V for Vendetta* who explodes the hypocrisy of Thatcherite England, the protagonist in "The Sentinel" from *Defenders of the Faith*, with its words of wisdom; "Tempt not the blade," and the cover of Judas Priest's *British Steel.*

⁹² **The stars of our work:** The beautiful last line of the poem draws a thread between Otto's earliest days and the present. Taken literally the stars are the ninja stars he spent so much time making as a boy taking his first shop class, taken more poetically the stars become the current poem and show the interconnectedness of Otto's life's work.

⁹² ὄττό εἶναι το πρᾶγμα που οι ἄνθρωποι αποκαλούν θεό.

GLOSSARY

Abyss calls, *Abyssus abyssum invocat*, "deep calleth unto deep,"
or "sea calls to sea," (Psalm 41) "It is there in the very depths
that the divine impact takes place, where the abyss of our
nothingness encounters the Abyss of mercy, the immensity of
the all, of God. There we will find the strength to die to ourselves
and, losing all vestige of self, we will be changed into love."
Elizabeth of the Trinity, *The Complete Works of Elizabeth of the
Trinity*, vol.1. See *Stars*.

Agency, the freedom that finds itself in ordered captivity where
imagination can transform into strength. See *Workshop*.

Agon, the Greek personification of conflict, struggle or contest. Agon
is the central concept of agon(y) in tragedy, shaped by the
fundamental characters of opposite positions, the protagonist
and antagonist. An inspiration to both political theorists and
designers, who, however, often fail to recognize the tragic
suffering at the heart of Agon's workings. As Normand Berlin
discusses in *The Secret Cause: A Discussion of Tragedy*, the cause
of tragic suffering "has been given names—God, gods, fate,
necessity, passion, blood—but no epithet adequately captures
the mystery. The secret cause remains secret—and this is the fact
tragedy forces us to acknowledge." See *Dis*.

Anarchism, practical self-organization, but could also refer to pre-
figurative LARPing of politics by critical elitists, See *Design*.

Anthropocene, a contemporary term that helps landscape painters
pay their bills, See *Luxury communism*.

Art, when Hamlet says to Horatio; "There are more things in Heaven
and Earth, Horatio, than are dreamt of in your philosophy."
See *Manowar*.

Babylon, may refer to one of the eight metal bands with this name,
from as diverse places as Italy, Japan, Malaysia, Mexico, and the
United States. See *Jerusalem*.

Brokkr and Sindri, Norse dwarves of Myrkheimr who forged many
magical items in Norse mythology, not least Thor's divine
hammer Mjölnir, but also Gleipnir, the thin chain made to bind
the demon wolf Fenrir until Ragnarok, the end of days. The
mythological chain was spun from the sound of a cat's footfall, the
beard of women, the roots of mountains, the sinews of the bear,
the breath of the fish, and the spittle of the birds. Since making
the chain, these things have been missing in the world, but will
return as the chain corrodes and ultimately breaks. See *Work*.

Center, epicenter as well as gravity well, gravitational pull of a large
body in space that affects attraction of objects, "the center / to
which all weight is drawn": "lo mezzo / al quale ogne gravezza si
rauna" (32:73-74), referring to Lucifer, once the most beautiful
of created beings who betrays his Creator, who appears in the

end, "you passed the point to which, from every part, all weights are drawn" : "tu passasti 'l punto / al qual si traggon d'ogne parte i pesi" (34:110-11). Even if inferno is below, Dante seems to contradict the Hollow Earth Theory. See *Ruin*.

Chymical, *Chymische Hochzeit Christiani Rosencreutz anno 1459,* an allegoric/esoteric romance divided into Seven Journeys of seven days. The manuscript appeared in Strasbourg in 1616. The English version, *Chymical Wedding of Christian Rosenkreutz,* was published in 1690, translated by esotericist Ezechiel Foxcroft. See *Love*.

Creativity, a clearly overrated aspect of design work, drawing its promise from cultural neophilia, prioritizing the "freshness" of ideas over the key attributes of design excellence according to Vitruvius: *firmitas, utilitas,* and *venustas,* or, strength, utility, and beauty. The emphasis on creativity tends to push aside other elements of design, such as empirical evaluation and iteration in accordance with use. This aspect becomes especially troublesome in "artistic research," which tends to mix the extractive practices of the art world with creative speculation and quick renderings, workshops, and interventions to demonstrate ideas safely embedded in vague but supportive discourse. The issue becomes apparent in Brian Massumi's much quoted foreword to Deleuze and Guattari's *Thousand Plateaus;*
> "The question is not, Is it true? But, Does it work? What new thoughts does it make possible to think? What new emotions does it make possible to feel? What new sensations and perceptions does it open in the body?"

It begs designers the question; Well, does it *work*? Perhaps someone thinks new thoughts, feels new emotions, and opens new sensations? So what? Does the world ask nothing more of design practice than the author getting feelings? See *Fabulation*.

Critical, grant-seeking shibboleth, or the language of etiquette that separates the professional non-profit class from the folks they manage. See *Despair*.

Darkness, dark/darkness mentioned 24 times in the cantos, may seem somewhat grim, but its meaning may range from the Stygian and crepuscular to the cryptic or esoteric. As Michael Wood reminds us in *The Magician's Doubts: Nabokov and the Risks of Fiction*, also Nabokov's *Pale Fire* "is light and funny in all kinds of marvelous ways, but we shall miss everything if we miss its darkness." See *Art*.

De Profundis, Psalm 130 (129 in the Vulgate) of the Book of Psalms, beginning with the words *De profundis clamavi ad te Domine;* "Out of the depths I have cried unto Thee, O Lord" A prayer of a sinner, trusting in the mercies of God.
The first few lines say;
> "Out of the depths I have cried unto Thee, O Lord;
> Lord, hear my voice. Let Thine ears be attentive to

the voice of my supplication.
If Thou, O Lord, shalt mark our iniquities: O Lord,
who can abide it?
For with Thee there is mercy: and by reason of Thy
law I have waited on Thee, O Lord.
My soul hath waited on His word: my soul hath
hoped in the Lord."
At the depths, the *mysterium tremendum*, that tremendous
mystery beyond human knowledge. May also refer to a song by
Watain on their 2013 album *The Wild Hunt*, See *Night*.

Death to false metal, according to metal mythos, was introduced
by Manowar in the first half of the 1980's. In this spirit,
Encyclopaedia Metallum, or the The Metal Archives, only
accepts bands that are "fully, unambiguously metal", thus not
Rock n' roll or metal-associated subgenres, such as glam, nu
metal, and other distortions of the lore. See *Manowar*.

Deed, "In the beginning was the Deed" is a line from Goethe's *Faust*,
where Faust states that our actions are the true manifestation of
our intentions and impact on the world, not what we wrote in
that paper a few PhD-students are forced to read. See *Speculation*.

Demiurge, in *Timaeus*, Plato describes the Demiurge as a divine
craftsman, an artisan, a divine carpenter, or more exactly, a
master carpenter who created the universe by imposing order
on chaos. The term was later adopted by some Gnostics, who
believed the Demiurge, or creator god, was a cunning and
deceptive force of evil, an imprisoning tyrant, trapping human
souls in the material realm and away from the higher truths
of thought and form. The goal of Gnosticism was to achieve
spiritual liberation from the prison of the Demiurge to reunite
with the true divine, and "one," source. As it is said; Death is only
the beginning. See *Babylon*.

Design, an inferno of saviors. See *Possibilism*.

Design thinking, a problem-solving process popularized across the
design field, dominating the discourse since the turn of the
century. The process focuses on the needs of the user, primarily
by emphasizing empathy between designer and user. In
combination with other popular theories, such as flat ontologies
and the politicization of the everyday, the method commonly
leads to either banal ideas and designs or, more commonly,
infantilization. See *Toxic Theory Shock Syndrome (TTSS)*.

Despair, a lucid journey of increasing possibilities, See *Night*.

Dis, "the city that bears the name of Dis" (Dante Canto 8:68),
consists of the sixth through the ninth circles of Hell. The name
is a contraction of *dives* (Latin "wealthy, rich"), short for Dis
Pater. Dis Pater, Rex Infernus, or Pluto, is a Roman god of the
underworld, which Dante refers to as Lucifer.

For Dante, Lucifer appears as the negator or oppositional
force; his attributes negate divine attributes because his being
is characterized only by what it is not. Lucifer was the most
beautiful of the angels with the greatest potential and virtue (the
name means "light bearer"), but in a bout of egotistical pride he
aspired to be greater than his maker, the sin that led to his fall.
His six wings are described as the banners of "the king of Hell":
"Vexilla regis prodeunt inferni" (34:1). To Dante, Lucifer's bat-
wings blow a freezing wind of un-love, instead of the biblical fire
and brimstone.

To Dante's pilgrims, Lucifer's body becomes the structure
of final transition through and out of Hell, as Earth's center of
gravity is an inversion and an axis around which the journey
pivots: what the travelers experienced as upside down, physically
and morally, is now turned around to show a new direction.
They climb on Lucifer's body, where after the hip bone, ("point
at which the thigh revolves, just at the swelling of the hip,")
the world turns, his legs now turned upwards, leaving Dante
perplexed. As they leave Hell, Dante asks; "Where is the ice? And
how is he so placed head downward?"

After climbing across Lucifer's body, they emerge on the
other side of earth, symbolizing Dante's movement away from sin
and his preparation for the coming journey through the terraces
of Purgatory, formed as the outside of Hell. This marks the end
of his pilgrimage through Hell and the beginning of the path
toward redemption. See *Center*.

Dis-ign, the disappointing disease and disaster of disillusionment
and disruption in dis time. Or the type of societal "engagement"
that epistemic elites claim to do as they turn their own toxic self-
improvement ideology into grant applications in the name of the
people. "The only successful philosophies and religions are the
ones that flatter us, whether in the name of progress or of hell.
Damned or not, man experiences an absolute need to be at the
heart of everything." Emil Cioran. See *Imperial mode of living.*

Dives and Lazarus, Dives, sometimes referred to as Dis, here a
parable of Jesus also called "The Rich man and Lazarus" (Luke
16:19-31), unique to Luke and thus not of the Q source. The
motif was popular in medieval art and poetry, and the parable
also is a traditional English folk song listed as Child ballad 56
and number 477 in the Roud Folk Song Index. In the story, the
rich man lives in luxury, ignoring Lazarus, a poor and sick beggar
at his gate. The rich man's sin is not explicit cruelty but his
indifference to Lazarus' suffering. After death, their situations
are reversed: Lazarus is comforted in Abraham's bosom, while
the rich man suffers eternal torment. The song dramatizes this
reversal to reinforce the medieval Christian teaching about divine
justice and the consequences of selfishness, urging listeners to
show compassion and charity to avoid Dives' fate. See also Richard
Crashaw, "Upon Lazarus His Tears" in *Steps to the Temple* (1646):
"Rich Lazarus! richer in those gems, thy tears,
Than Dives in the robes he wears:

> He scorns them now, but oh they'll suit full well
> With the purple he must wear in hell."

The emphasis on belief appears across popular design discourse today, and runs deep in the thinking classes. As observed by Mark Fisher, "so long as we believe (in our hearts) that capitalism is bad, we are free to continue in capitalist exchange," and another example may be the belief that carefully chosen words can overturn oppression. See *Interrogate*.

Divine Hammer, "Justice divine doth smite them with its hammer." in Dante's Canto XI:90, Virgil references Aristotle's *Ethic* with the image of a divine tool to punish bestiality beyond malice, or anonymous peer-reviewers promoting their own texts to gain citations. See *Hellhammer*.

Dreams, a recurring thread through the cantos, but emphasized in Canto II. Designers dream of something meaningful, but not necessarily real, not unlike how androids dream of electric sheep, and replicants dream of being humans. Obvious reference to *Blade Runner* (1982), and the sequel *Blade Runner 2049* (2017). The sequel, at several points, engages Vladimir Nabokov's novel *Pale Fire* (1962). In the movie, lines from the poem *Pale Fire* are used in the Post-Trauma Baseline Test, which the replicant K takes to assess his humanity. The lines include "Cells interlinked within cells interlinked / Within one stem" and "And dreadfully distinct / Against the dark, a tall white fountain played".

In Nabokov's book, Shade's poem starts with the lines:
> "I was the shadow of the waxwing slain
> By the false azure in the windowpane;
> I was the smudge of ashen fluff—and I
> Lived on, flew on, in the reflected sky."

Shade, as a human being, dead already from the news of his daughter's suicide, is a shadow of himself, killed by smashing himself against the transparent but deadly glass pane of reality, smudged, yet keeps on living as a mere reflection. In an obvious transference, the replicants in Blade Runner are robots who dream of being like humans, striving for meaning, yet can never be sure what that desire is, or where it comes from, or what it might mean. This becomes even more poignant as humans are not necessarily portrayed in a favorable light in the movie's not-so-distant-future. Taken as a textbook warning of the future predicted by Ivan Illich, the inhabitants of the future are themselves smudged against a dystopian reality of over-designed, convenient and inherently technocratic meaninglessness, but seem to dream of vividly projected commodities.

Compare to "Dreams Never End," the opening track on New Order's 1981 album *Movement*, the first after Ian Curtis' death and the break up of Joy Division. The song's title answers to Ian Curtis' words in "Insight" from *Unknown Pleasures*, itself a comment on Dante's *Inferno* ("Guess your dreams always end. They don't rise up, just descend"), but here the lyrics initiate a

new chapter (or order) for the band. The opening lines, sung
by Peter Hook, highlights how dreams are caught in conflicts
between visions and promises and are not harmless fabulations;

"My promise could be your fiend
A given end to your dreams
A simple movement or rhyme
Could be the smallest of signs"

If you still have some, <u>see</u> *Hope.*

Empathy, design acrobatics to cloud judgment. "If we could truly see
ourselves the way others see us we'd disappear on the spot." Emil
Cioran. <u>See</u> *Design thinking.*

Entombed, entombments are typically burials above ground, placing
the body within a crypt, tomb, mausoleum, or columbarium,
which is then sealed. Referenced in Dante as the Last Judgment,
as eternity replaces temporal categories, "graves will be closed
down" and where the Epicureans (Canto X) will be physically
and mentally entombed in their ways, cut off from the world,
turned inwards and against themselves. Compare with the heresy
of design, to lock oneself in the dark echo of self-reference. Just
think of Timon's bitter epitaph he wrote for himself appears as
the last strophes of Shakespeare's *Timon of Athens* (1606/1623);

"Here lies a wretched corpse of wretched soul bereft:
Seek not my name: a plague consume you wicked
caitiffs left!
Here lie I, Timon, who alive, all living men did hate,
Pass by, and curse thy fill, but pass and stay not here
thy gait."

Also a genre defining Swedish death metal band formed in 1987.
<u>See</u> *Hellhammer.*

Eternal Fire, if not seen as an image of hell, this could refer to
the fenix fire of rebirth and the Bardo, the intermediate,
transitional, or liminal state between death and rebirth, a gap in
our perception of reality caused by the dissolution of the body,
filled with harrowing and terrifying visions, and a moment
for transformation. It is sometimes referred to as a fire of
cleansing, preparing the soul for rebirth. *The Bardo Thödol*, or
Tibetan Book of the Dead, primarily describes three bardos: the
Chikhai, Chonyid, and *Sidpa* bardos. The *Chikhai* bardo is the
experience at the moment of death. The *Chonyid* bardo is the
experience of seeing visions of Buddha forms. The *Sidpa* bardo
is the experience of visions that lead to rebirth, a hell desperately
needed in design today.

The notion of the "Eternal Fire" points to the journey
of suffering explored in the song "Enter the Eternal Fire" on
Bathory's pivotal black metal album of 1987, *Under the Sign of
the Black Mark*. Here, Quorthon follows a protagonist as they
must suffer the eternal fire for a deal made with the Devil; "The
price now I must pay for eternity my soul his claim, For years of
pleasures, victory and gold."

Seen through the lens of Chögyam Trungpa's notion of "spiritual materialism," Quorthon's protagonist now pays for the years of self-deceptive gluttony that is not primarily physical but spiritual, representing an overindulgence in the pursuit of bliss and transcendence without restraint, and where the quest for spiritual revelation has become yet another service and object to consume (the "pleasures, victory and gold" that comes with an abundance of yoga retreats, mindfulness workshops, and athleisure). ˢᵉᵉ *Abyss.*

Ethics, in design, most often referring to elite sentimentality coded as philosophy. Compare with how Brecht phrases it in *The Threepenny Opera*; "What is robbing a bank compared to founding a bank?" A more generous take could be how John D. Caputo puts it; "It is not a question of finding an answer to the night of truth," he argues in *Against Ethics*, "but of sitting up with one another through the night, of dividing the abyss in half in a companionship that is its own meaning." ˢᵉᵉ *Journey.*

Fabulation, a literary and designerly style that combines realistic elements with magical, fantastic, or surreal elements. Also, a mental health condition where someone tells invented stories that they believe are true, or believe can come true by mere thinking. Fabulations are frequently suggested in connection to cultural critic Frederic Jameson's much attributed quote that "it's easier to imagine the end of the world than the end of capitalism." This delusional statement is often made in connection to Mark Fischer's notion of *Hauntology*, the culture of lost futures and post-capitalist desires under late capitalism. As fabulation requires nothing more than minute imagination, and lacks any defining qualities to critique, it has become a prevalent refuge amongst spineless designers who try to escape empirical reality checks. ˢᵉᵉ *Deed.*

Fecundity, the overkill of design and human intention to subdue the world following God's command to Adam and Eve to "Be fruitful, multiply, fill the earth, and subdue it," from Latin *fēcunditās*, 'fruitfulness' or 'fertility,' see the work of H.P. Lovecraft, or the chapter with the same name in *Pilgrim at Tinker Creek* by Annie Dillard (1974). ˢᵉᵉ *Darkness.*

Fire, mentioned six times in the cantos. ˢᵉᵉ *Sicilian bull.*

Hades, "Whoever descends into Hades uninitiated and unpurified shall grovel in the mire; but he who has been purified and initiated shall on his arrival there dwell with the gods." Iamblichus *The Exhortation to Philosophy*. Also, the opening song on Bathory's first full length album. ˢᵉᵉ *Eternal Fire.*

Hammer, could be the hammer of Thor, Hercules, Nietzsche, Brecht, or Ilmarinen, or the *Hexenhammer*, hinting at labor with impact. Many designers may think of *Uchide no kozuchi* (jap. lit. "Tap-Appear Mallet"), a mythological magic hammer which can "tap out" anything wished for. This magic wooden hammer is a standard token held in the hand of the deity of fortune, fertility, and wealth, Daikoku-ten. See *Brokkr and Sindri.*

Hellhammer, a Swiss extreme metal band from Nürensdorf, active from 1982 to 1984. As the band disbanded, guitarist/vocalist Thomas Gabriel Fischer and bassist/vocalist Urs Sprenger went on to form the influential band Celtic Frost. See *Abyss.*

Hellmouth, "what goes into Hellmouth almost never comes out the other end. Shit happens a lot in Hell, but infernal shit never actually gets flushed away. It just collects" James Miller states in *Dante and the Unorthodox: The Aesthetics of Transgression.* Compare with Canto 28: 25-27,
> "Between the legs the entrails dangled. I saw
> the innards and the loathsome sack
> that turns what one has swallowed into shit."

Or, consider that Andres Serrano was invited to the Sistine Chapel by Pope Francis in 2023, even though Serrano's work is on the cover of Metallica's *Load* and *Reload* albums, infernal shit far worse than *Piss Christ.* See *Art.*

Heresy, the willful self-separation of the soul from God, or from the purpose of life. For Dante, the heretics' souls are "buried within those sarcophagi" — "seppelite dentro da quell'arche" (9:125). They are thus buried in tombs of disbelief, signifying their willful turning away from the life of truth. A similar fate may await self-centered designers. See *Tertullian.*

Hope, mentioned 23 times in the cantos. An active effort of disciplined practice, continuously starting over, often against one's knowledge of long defeat. But also, "hope is optimism with a broken heart," as Nick Cave says instead of rage-quitting. See *Progress.*

Hypokrisis, from Greek, *hypokritēs* "actor on a stage, pretender," but also, *yper* (above) *crisis* (gold), To Dante, the hypocrites are placed lower in hell than murderers as their effects are more insidious and ultimately more damaging to the social fabric. Thus the hypocrites literally bear the tonnage of their own hypocrisy. Consider how "each tree is known by its own fruit." (Luke 6:43-44) See *Design thinking.*

Ice, a mirror. See *Silence.*

Imperial mode of living, the dominant lifestyle of people of the Global North, named so, *imperiale Lebensweise,* by German sociologists Ulrich Brand and Markus Wissen. Designed to be a convenient standard of living, it is made possible, desirable, and accessible by design. While empowering people's everyday practices, orientations and identities, it is a mode of living that normalizes the extraction and exploitation inherent in its functioning, making all participants dependent and complicit in its continuing operation. By being attractive and possibly accessible to the excluded, it ties the hopes of the poor to not overthrow imperial conditions but to participate in its exclusive privileges. Conveniently designed and priced commodities may come to mind, while fashion may be one of its foremost manifestations. See *Design.*

Interrogate, one-way discourse to avoid being questioned, making a meme-designer feel like Che Guevara. See *Fabulation.*

Irene, or Eirene, (Greek; Peace), is one of the *Horae,* the personification and goddess of peace in Greek mythology, particularly well regarded by the citizens of Athens. Her Roman equivalent is the goddess Pax. See *Workshop.*

Jerusalem, Saint Augustine formed the idea of a universal religious city or community: "Just as there is only one holy city – Jerusalem – so there is only one city of iniquity – Babylon. All the wicked [souls] belong to Babylon just as all the godly ones belong to Jerusalem." (Enarr. in Ps., 86). Compare with Tertullian, early Church father, who famously asked, "What hath Athens to do with Jerusalem?" a discussion furthered by political theorist Leo Strauss' suggestion how western ideologies emerge out of Jerusalem and Athens as the coming together of biblical faith and Greek thought to shape the values of modern Western culture. See *Babylon.*

Journey, a dark road of scars that may not make us comfortable or ease our pain. The unknowable spiritual annihilation of all one believed in and thought one was. The state of respite mentioned in *The Dark Night of the Soul;*

> "In darkness and secure,
> By the secret ladder, disguised
> —oh, happy chance!—
> In darkness and in concealment,
> My house being now at rest."

Can be compared with *Kenosis,* (Greek lit. 'the act of emptying') the self-emptying of one's own will, where the process of emptying opens a person for divine grace in union with God. See *Pilgrim.*

Justice, in *Pale Fire,* notice how Kinbote presses Shade on the question of God: "Who is the judge of life, and the Designer of death?" See *Empathy.*

Love, mentioned twice; first as missing, then as misled. As Simone Weil posits, love is not consolation, it is light. Consider William Shakespeare's words in *Timon of Athens;* "The moon's an arrant thief, And her pale fire she snatches from the sun." See *Fire.*

Luxury communists, highlighting the trouble of serving both God and Mammon, (Matthew 6:24), or, here's another way to think about it; the weak serve the strong to get fed. If you do not produce to support yourself through the means of market exchange, you become dependent on political means. And under this dependency, you need to align with their political values so you get your handouts. The better you align, the better handouts, and the more dependent you become. See *Interrogate*.

Making, "If all things are parts of god, then all things are god, and he makes himself in making things. His making can never cease because he is ceaseless. And as god has no end, so his making has neither beginning nor end." *Corpus Hermeticum*. XVI.18. See *Hammer*.

Manowar, an American heavy metal band from Auburn, New York, formed in 1980 that shows appreciation for the forge. The 1984 "Sign of the hammer" suggests;
>"The spell has been broken, the curse has been lifted
>Black is the wind on the heels of the gifted [...]
>Onward pounding into glory ride
>Sign of the hammer be my guide
>Final warning, all stand aside
>Sign of the hammer it's my time"

"Do not abuse matter, for it is not dishonorable." St John of Damascus, *Three Treatises on the Divine Images*. See *Ruin*.

Marx's coat, read the essay with the same name by Peter Stallybrass. Discuss.

Massive Change, an influential book in the field of design, *Massive Change: The Future of Global Design* by Bruce Mau (Phaidon, 2004), is suggestively "not about the world of design, it's about the design of the world." The book aims to "chart the bewildering complexity of our increasingly interconnected (and designed) world," giving a wide overview of designed systems globally. The book's broad scope examines how global design taps into "global commons," to "distribute capacity," and "embrace paradox" while also redesigning Third World property law.

The ideas behind the book are inspired by British historian Arnold J. Toynbee (1889-1975), who proposed a circular motility of civilizations, which rise when they respond to challenges with the help of creative minorities or groups of elite leaders (designers anyone?), and decline when their leaders fail to respond creatively, which leads to the civilization's fall by revolts and entailing tyranny. To quote point eight in Bruce Mau's famous *Incomplete Manifesto for Growth*; "Lack judgment. Postpone criticism." See *Design thinking*.

Maze, when the labyrinth of life turns full of crossroads, each of which leads to hell. See *Pilgrim*.

Night, spiritual dryness, desolation, possible purification, the seed that fell on the rocks. See *Journey*.

Nudging, subtle behavioral prompts to push users to follow the decrees of the client, ranging from uncalled advice all the way to violence. A contemporary interpretation of Arnold Geulincx' *Ubi* *nihil vales, ibi nihil velis,* "Wherein you have no power, therein neither should you will." See *Dis-ign.*

Occam, William of Ockham, or Gulielmus Occamus (c. 1287 – 1347), English Franciscan, famous for his methodologically sharp blade and dexterity to cut the crap. See *Deed.*

Omphalos, Greek "navel," the idea that Delphi was the center of the world, what the Romans called, *umbilicus mundi,* or "navel of the world." May also refer to the marble section called the Omphalion on the floor in the Hagia Sophia, consisting of 30 circles of various sizes and colors, marking the spot of Byzantine coronations. Also denoting the implosion and ever inward centripetal crunch of individualism and the consumer immunity paradigm that guides mainline design practices. Could also refer to the navel-gazing prevalent amongst the NGO-classes as they build their own CVs in the name of "community." See *Selfhood.*

Opium, or, Opium-eaters, the opium points to design being the sigh of the oppressed creature, the heart of a heartless world, and the soul of our soulless conditions. Or as political philosopher John Gray points out;

> "Contemporary capitalism promises its labourers a better life on earth in a mythical future in which no one any longer believes. In feudal societies, serfs were drugged in acquiescence by a spiritual opiate. In the most advanced liberal society, the underclass dies of fentanyl."

However, in Canto II, the term probably points to Thomas De Quincey's *Confessions of an English Opium-Eater* of 1821/1822, where De Quincey exposes how to "dream magnificently," with the assistance of the drug, and he later, in *Suspiria De Profundis,* further expands on how to use opium to develop the "dreaming organ" to "assist the faculty of dreaming" as it is not merely "exalting the colors of dream-scenery, but for deepening its shadows; and, above all, for strengthening the sense of its fearful *realities.*" De Quincey asks himself; "But how came you to dream more splendidly than others?" And he answers himself; "Because *(praemissis praemittendis)* I took excessive quantities of opium."

De Quincy places his confessions in reference to the Lotus-eaters, or the "Lotophagi," in Homer's *Odyssey,* Book IX, who eat the fruit of the lotos, which is "sweet as honey." After they ate the lotus, they would forget their home and loved ones and long only to stay with their fellow lotus-eaters. Those who ate the plant never cared to report or return, but remained passive and docile, indulging in pleasure, luxury, and the latest issue of Monocle. See *Dreams.*

Pilgrim, from Latin *peregrinus* 'foreign' and Provençal *pelegrin,* - late Middle English: from Latin *peregrinus* 'foreign', from *peregre* 'abroad', from *per-* 'through' + *ager* 'field'. Compare the journey of Dante and Virgil with that described in *The Pilgrimage of the Soul* (or *The Pylgremage of the Sowle*) "Progress sounds the call to Duty, and the Child the Man obeys". See *Jerusalem.*

Pitch deck, speculative tool for beggars, popularly used by the paupers of the creative classes, ^{See} *Fabulation.*

Plain Zero, ^{see} *The Running Man* (1987)

Political, gaslighting the garbage in Sodom and Gomorrah. ^{See} *Justice.*

Possbilism, the theory in geography that human behaviour and culture are not merely determined by the environment but that human agency has the power to shape the environment. Opposed to geographic determinism. Seen through the lens of design, possibilism supports the fantasy of the sovereign user in order to cover for the underlying anxiety about their real lack of agency in the world. ^{See} *De profundis.*

Problem/Predicament, tension appearing when designers take on civilizational paradoxes without the faintest shadow of solving, or even addressing, them. Instead, they set out to "frame" such issues. Often these topics come in a combination of "addressing the climate challenge", "following the science", and "saving the planet," set out as design challenges but without recognizing design itself being the problem. ^{See} *Design thinking.*

Progress, a faith in design's liberating power with a continuous renewal of eschatological hope towards unlimited perfection. A process through which "all that is holy is profaned," as Marx has it. Or, seen from a different perspective; "Progress consists, not in the increase of truth, but in freeing it from its wrappings. The truth is obtained like gold, not by letting it grow bigger, but by washing off from it everything that isn't gold." Leo Tolstoy: *Diaries,* ^{See} *Chymical.*

Rise, as St. Augustine posits; "Do you wish to rise? Begin by descending. You plan a tower that will pierce the clouds? Lay first the foundation of humility." ^{See} *Abyss calls.*

Ruin, in Dante, hell is only possible because of the *Ruina*, a landslide fracture of its concentric structure caused by the Crucifixion. This is the feature of the lustful curse in *Inferno's* Canto V: "When they come before the landslide, there the shrieks, the wailing, the lamenting; there they curse God's power." ^{See} *Love.*

Salomon, could also be Suleyman, Solomon, Salman, as well as a reference to Otto Aron Salomon (1849–1907), the Swedish educator, writer and proponent of educational sloyd. Started by Uno Cygnaeus (1810-1888), a Finnish clergyman and educator, the pedagogic system of sloyd (Swedish *slöjd*) is a handicraft-based education model introduced to public school curriculum in the latter part of the 1800s. Originally inspired by the educational philosophers Johann Heinrich Pestalozzi and Friedrich Fröbel, the system was further developed by Salomon at the Sloyd Teachers Seminary in Nääs, Sweden, from where he popularized the educational sloyd movement with students from across the world. The sloyd system became the model for shop class and other embodied and practically infused forms of learning in public education, and still plays an essential part of Scandinavian public education. See *Making.*

Secret, something hidden, or unspeakable, or unknowable, not unlike how we cannot know exactly what Meat Loaf won't do for love. Or a reference to *Secretum Secretorum,* (Lat. "Secret of Secrets") also known as the *Sirr al-Asrar.* A pseudo-Aristotelian work, supposedly a letter from Aristotle to his student Alexander the Great, that first emerged in the 9th century. Often the later 13th-century edition is referred to as it includes several alchemical references as well as an early version of the Emerald Tablet. See *Chymical.*

Selfhood, a metamorphosis, See *Silence.*

Sicilian bull, also in Dante 27:7, the brazen bull, or bronze bull, or bull of Phalaris, was a torture and execution device designed in ancient Greece. The hollow bull, with a small door, had a fire set beneath it, slowly roasting the victim inside to death. The screams of the dying were said to sound like the bellows of a bull. According to legend, Perilaus invented and presented the device to Phalaris, the tyrant of Akragas, Sicily, who then had Perilaus executed within his invention. Later, when Phalaris was overthrown, he also came to experience the interior of the bull. Thus the creator becomes the victim of his clever device. Blessed be the forgers of iron.

Silence, Ivan Illich: "silence, according to western and eastern tradition alike, is necessary for the emergence of persons." Furthermore, "just as clean air makes it possible to breathe," craft proponent Matthew Crawford notes in *The New York Times* in 2015, "silence makes it possible to think." Stay with the hand tools. See *Virtue of silence.*

Simony, the ecclesiastical crime of paying or using family connections to obtain ecclesiastical offices or positions. In Dante's *Inferno,* the Eighth Circle of Hell (canto 19) is reserved for those who committed simony. The Simoniacs are placed headfirst in holes, flames burning on the soles of their feet. See *Subzero.*

Sleep, in every man there sleeps a designer, and when he wakes there is a little more evil in the world. See *Dis-ign.*

Solomon, in the Bible, King Solomon, the son of God, is known for his wisdom (Hebrew, *Chokmah*). Chokmah is the ability to make the right choices at the right time, untangling knotted dilemmas, and it is a skill that comes from God. In Kabbalah, Chokmah is the second of the ten sefirot in the Tree of Life, the uppermost part of the right pillar, Jachin. Some of Solomon's wisdom was later encrypted in the enigmatic lock-picking grimoire *Greater*

Key of Solomon, a source of practical wisdom as well as esoteric and magic transformation. ^{See} *Secret.*

Speculation, illusionist daydreaming amongst bogus-radicals setting out to "challenge the status quo" by provoking their own bias. ^{See} *Death to false metal.*

Stars, in Dante, after finding their way up, the travelers return to the world of light and to the stars: "and so we emerged, to see — once more — the stars" : "E quindi uscimmo a riveder le stelle" (34:139).

Subzero, ^{See} *Plain Zero.*

Tertullian, or Quintus Septimius Florens Tertullianus (c. 155 – c. 220), early Christian author from Carthage, sometimes called "the father of Latin Christianity," and seen as one of the founders of Western theology. Tertullian suggests the Scriptures' warning of "vain" philosophy meant all philosophy, where their very mode of thinking formed the foundation of heresies in early Christianity and, therefore, should be avoided. To Tertullian, instruction comes from 'the porch of Solomon,' who had himself taught that 'the Lord should be sought in simplicity of heart.' ^{See} *Virtues.*

Toxic Theory Shock Syndrome (TTSS), signifies a state of profound anxiety, mental haze, and paralyzing shock to the agency of the victim. Central to the concept is the degree to which a particular mixture of theoretical approaches can damage the functioning of an organism and cause severe debilitation and depression. The toxicant's effects depend on dose and combination; even harmless ideas can lead to damage when taken in too high a dose or in combination with other ideas. A recurring toxic mixture amongst designers seems to come from flat ontologies meeting pan-politicization. ^{See} *Hellmouth.*

Tradition, the power of empiricism and limits, the rigidity that leverages effort to strength. Compare with Edmund Burke's famous quote; "You began ill, because you began by despising everything that belonged to you." Consider Hannah Arendt's essay "Tradition and the Modern Age." ^{See} *Hammer.*

Virgil, is legion, a figure of many faces, not least the ring name of American professional WWF wrestler Michael Charles Jones (1951–2024), who in 1988 assisted Andre The Giant's infamous "event," beating Hulk Hogan, which many fans argue Dante foresaw. Also Publius Vergilius Maro (70-19 BCE), born near Mantua in Cisalpine Gaul, author of three famous texts in Latin literature: the *Eclogues* (or *Bucolics*), the *Georgics*, and the epic *Aeneid.* In the *Inferno,* Virgil appears as a guide to Dante's journey through hell, and is often interpreted as representing the natural light of reason. Virgil was revered by Dante as the greatest of poets, and in canto VIII, Dante addresses Virgil with the words, "Beata colei che in te s'incise!" (Proud soul, blessed is she who conceived thee!"), a passage that clearly echoes the gospel concerning the Virgin Mary: "Beatus venter qui te portavit" (Blessed is the womb that bare thee [Jesus]", Luke, 11:27). It is unclear what Dante would think of the blackened deathcore band that now bears his idol's name. See *The Great Escape* where Steve McQueen plays Virgil.

Virtues, to Dante, the virtues refer to the four cardinal virtues: Prudence, Justice, Temperance, and Fortitude. The "cardinal" comes from *cardo*, Latin for "hinge," or the axis around which the world rotates. In Dante's descent, notice how the journey turns on the hinge of Lucifer's hip, frozen at the surface of the ice, where the body turns into the stairs they can ascend upwards again. Thomas of Aquinas famously discussed the three theological virtues: Faith, Hope and Charity. See *Abyss calls*.

Virtue of silence, a space to listen to the subtle messages of the soul, intuition, or divine guidance, or sometimes even people. As stated in the *Corpus Hermeticum*; "In the moment when you have nothing to say about it, you will see it, for the knowledge of it is divine silence, and suppression of all senses." A different interpretation is that of *Apophasis*, a rhetorical device translated as "unsaying", where the speaker or writer speaks of a silence, for example, by bringing up a subject by denying it should be brought up, or using negation, as in negative theology; we can only get a hint about God by what it is not, such as cobbler and mystic Jakob Böhme's statement that "God is the un-ground of reality." Absence of performative projection, See *Chymical*.

Voice/Noise, the performative verbiage that, perhaps paradoxically, turns voice into noise, in an inversion of Jacques Rancière's politics of speech. See *Agon*.

Work, may refer to vastly divergent types of practices, from "doing the work" of the non-profit class, to Dion Fortune's notion that practice must "train the mind, not inform it," that is, to train the attention, attitude and skills towards agency. Could also refer to the dignity of work, today often labelled "craft," that is to be rationalized away by design processes favoring efficiency and user-friendliness, See *Deed*.

Workshop, a temple, a place of both labor and rest. As it is said in *The Book of Privy Counseling,* the second part of *The Cloud of Unknowing* of the 14th century; "Knowledge tends to breed conceit, but love builds. Knowledge is full of labor, but love, full of rest." See *Rise*.

I have made an end at last,
and my weary hand can rest.

COLOPHON

Set Margins' number: #59

The Design Comedy
The Descent Through Inferno

Author: Otto von Busch
Foreword: Nicola Masciandaro
Commentary: Aaron Sechler

ISBN: 978-90-834993-6-9

Graphic design: Eric de Haas
Illustrations: Gustave Doré's illustrations
                    to Dante's Inferno, ravaged by Otto.

Printer: Printon
Fonts: Miller Text, Aktiv Grotesk

Thanks to my Beatrices; Evren, Aurora, and Orion,
who bring light to even the darkest corners.

This publication is licensed under a Creative Commons
Attribution-NonCommercial-ShareAlike 4.0 International
Licence (CC BY-NC-SA 4.0). To view a copy of this license,
visit https://creativecommons.org/licenses/by-nc-sa/4.0/

First edition, 2025
Set Margins'

www.setmargins.press